MASTER POINT PRESS | TORONTO

POSITIVE DEFENSE at bridge

D1262019

TERENCE REESE & JULIAN POTTAGE

Master Point Press
331 Douglas Ave.
Toronto, Ontario, Canada
M5M 1H2
(416) 781-0351
Website: http://www.masterpointpress.com
Email: info@masterpointpress.com

Library and Archives Canada Cataloguing in Publication

Reese, Terence
    Positive defense / Terence Reese & Julian Pottage. -- Rev. ed.

ISBN 1-894154-93-2

    1. Contract bridge--Defensive play. I. Pottage, Julian II. Title.

GV1282.42.R43 2005   795.41'53   C2004-906796-6

Editor   Ray Lee
Cover and interior design   Olena S. Sullivan/New Mediatrix
Interior format   Luise Lee
Copy editing   Suzanne Hocking

Printed in Canada by Webcom Ltd.

1 2 3 4 5 6 7   09 08 07 06 05

Introduction

Many bridge players, if they are honest, admit that they find defending difficult and some say that the deals they misdefend return to haunt them in their dreams. Fortunately, this need not be the case. If you make a little effort — thinking logically, taking a little time to work out what declarer's plan is and what you can do to counteract it — you will find yourself defeating more contracts. Of course, developing an awareness of the things to look out for, a sense of intuition, takes time and practice, and that is what this book is about.

A few of the problems, if you managed to solve them at the table, would win you a prize for brilliance. The vast majority, however, are within the grasp of anyone with a sound grounding in bridge technique and the willingness to spend a few minutes searching for the right play.

There are two ways of approaching a book of this kind. The first is to treat each deal as a puzzle, only turning to the solution when you are confident that you cannot improve upon your answer. The second is to take as much time as you think would be reasonable at the table. Either way you will learn how to think along the right lines, which is what counts in this game.

Unless otherwise stated you may assume a rubber bridge setting. This means that you can forget about stopping overtricks and that you can assume simple bidding as well as standard leads and signals. What we have normally done where a deal comes from actual play is to preserve the original sequence. Anything out of the ordinary, we shall point out as we go along.

Terence Reese 1985
Julian Pottage 2005

Acknowledgments

For their part in inspiring this book, in accepting it for original publication, and for introducing Terence Reese and Julian Pottage to each other, the authors are indebted to Richard Plackett, Peter Crawley and Patrick Jourdain respectively.

For enabling this new, expanded and improved edition to appear in print, the authors also owe their gratitude to William Bailey, Peter Burrows, Maureen Dennison, Ron Garber, Mark Horton, Ray Lee and Alwyn Reese.

Contents

Opening Exchange

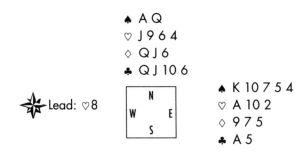

♠ A Q
♡ J 9 6 4
◇ Q J 6
♣ Q J 10 6

Lead: ♡8

♠ K 10 7 5 4
♡ A 10 2
◇ 9 7 5
♣ A 5

Dealer South
Neither vul.

WEST	NORTH	EAST	SOUTH
			1NT[1]
pass	2♣	pass	2◇
pass	3NT	all pass	

1. 12-14

South's 1NT is 12-14. North's Stayman 2♣, with his values in all the suits, seems highly dubious but that's the way of the world. In order for a 4-4 heart fit to produce game when 3NT would fail, it would need to yield two extra tricks, which is only likely to occur if the declaring side has a weak suit or two ruffs are possible. Also, if no fit comes to light, the defenders will have an easier task when they know about declarer's major-suit lengths.

West leads the ♡8, presumably top of nothing from three small, and dummy plays low. How should you, as East, plan to beat the contract?

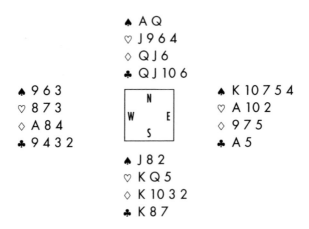

♠ A Q
♡ J 9 6 4
♢ Q J 6
♣ Q J 10 6

♠ 9 6 3
♡ 8 7 3
♢ A 8 4
♣ 9 4 3 2

♠ K 10 7 5 4
♡ A 10 2
♢ 9 7 5
♣ A 5

♠ J 8 2
♡ K Q 5
♢ K 10 3 2
♣ K 8 7

West leads the eight of hearts against 3NT and dummy plays low.

You would have been happier with a spade lead but you should give partner some credit for trying to find your suit; presumably he has similar holdings in the majors and guessed wrongly this time. There are still chances, however, because there is room for partner to hold the ◇A. Even the ♣K would be good enough in some circumstances, though partner would need four diamonds as well. In any case, you must win and attack spades even though it means leading into the tenace. No matter which minor declarer chooses to attack first, one of the defenders will win at once and persevere with spades. Either way, you can hold him to eight tricks: two spades, three hearts and three tricks in the minor he attacks first.

If dummy had held ♠A-K, and you had ♠Q-x-x-x-x then you would hardly have paused for a moment before winning with the ♡A and returning a spade.

Excess Baggage

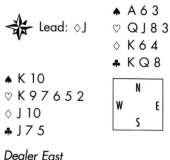

```
          ♠ A 6 3
🟊 Lead: ◇J    ♡ Q J 8 3
          ◇ K 6 4
          ♣ K Q 8

♠ K 10
♡ K 9 7 6 5 2     N
◇ J 10        W       E
♣ J 7 5           S
```

Dealer East
Both vul.

WEST	NORTH	EAST	SOUTH
		pass	3♠
pass	3NT	pass	4♠
all pass			

North may have bid 3NT with the idea of protecting his ◇K, but South persisted with his long suit, as players tend to do. To bid 3NT, North should have either a source of tricks of his own or sufficient support for spades to expect the suit to run.

You start with the ◇J; this choice turns out well as it holds the trick. You continue with the ◇10; your partner overtakes with the ◇Q and lays down the ◇A, declarer still following suit.

What should you play on the third round of diamonds?

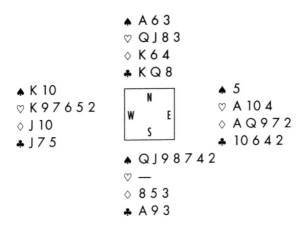

                          ♠ A 6 3
                          ♡ Q J 8 3
                          ◇ K 6 4
                          ♣ K Q 8
    ♠ K 10   ♠ 5
    ♡ K 9 7 6 5 2   ┌─────────┐   ♡ A 10 4
    ◇ J 10   W │   N   │ E   ◇ A Q 9 7 2
    ♣ J 7 5   │   S   │   ♣ 10 6 4 2
                       └─────────┘
                          ♠ Q J 9 8 7 4 2
                          ♡ —
                          ◇ 8 5 3
                          ♣ A 9 3

Your lead of the jack of diamonds holds the first trick. When you continue with the ten, partner overtakes with the queen and cashes the ace.

You must not sit back thinking: 'If partner has an ace, he'll cash it and I may make a spade trick as well.' You can be certain that a fourth diamond will establish the setting trick. Don't give partner any scope to do the wrong thing. Discard the king of hearts on the third diamond. After learned thought he will lead a fourth diamond and you will be able to relax. If declarer ruffs high, look the other way; otherwise, insert the ♠10 to force dummy's ace.

If a defender leads a suit of which the other three players are void, other trump layouts can be vulnerable to attack:

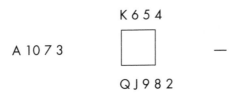

                    K 6 5 4
                  ┌─────────┐
    A 10 7 3   │   │   —
                  └─────────┘
                    Q J 9 8 2

Here West threatens to ruff with the seven and declarer is caught between the devil and the deep blue sea.

Watch the Little Birdie

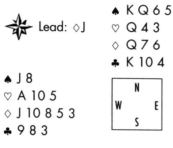

⚹ Lead: ◊J

♠ K Q 6 5
♡ Q 4 3
◊ Q 7 6
♣ K 10 4

♠ J 8
♡ A 10 5
◊ J 10 8 5 3
♣ 9 8 3

```
        N
  W         E
        S
```

Dealer South
Both vul.

WEST	NORTH	EAST	SOUTH
			1♡
pass	1♠	pass	2♡
pass	4♡	all pass	

With no aces and no ruffing value, North's jump to 4♡ seems marginal. Still, the lure of trying for a vulnerable game bonus (or to clinch the rubber) is hard to resist and can put added pressure on the defenders. Also, North can reasonably place South with a six-card heart suit.

You lead the ◊J and the ◊Q, the ◊K and the ◊A all cover this. Declarer cashes the ♠A, partner playing the ♠3, and then leads the ♡6.

What is your plan at this point?

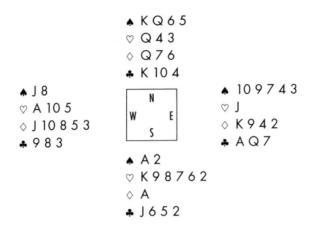

```
              ♠ K Q 6 5
              ♡ Q 4 3
              ◇ Q 7 6
              ♣ K 10 4
♠ J 8                          ♠ 10 9 7 4 3
♡ A 10 5         N             ♡ J
◇ J 10 8 5 3   W   E           ◇ K 9 4 2
♣ 9 8 3          S             ♣ A Q 7
              ♠ A 2
              ♡ K 9 8 7 6 2
              ◇ A
              ♣ J 6 5 2
```

You lead the jack of diamonds, covered by the queen, king and ace. Declarer cashes the ace of spades, your partner playing the three, and then declarer leads a low heart from hand.

Did you by any chance say to yourself: 'Does he think I'm going to let him get to dummy with the queen of hearts and discard a diamond on the king of spades? I'm going to take the ace of hearts and ten of diamonds, and then try for a couple of tricks in clubs.'

This analysis contains one serious flaw. Your partner played the ♠3 under the ace. If he was too lazy to play a higher card from a six-card suit then he must take the blame. Perhaps the ◇Q was a cunning play by your opponent and the ♠A another small deception. So duck the heart. When you come in with the ♡10, switch to the ♣9 and let partner decide what to do.

Declarer could have made the contract by starting trumps from dummy (or by laying down the king). However, he had no reason to place you with trump length. Although you may have seen through his little ruse, it would have worked against many West players.

Not So Foolish

```
            ♠ A 6 5 3 2
            ♡ K J 8
            ◊ K Q 5
            ♣ 4 2
                          ┌─────────┐      ♠ K Q 8
  ✦ Lead: ♣8              │    N    │      ♡ Q 10 4 2
                          │  W   E  │      ◊ 10 9 6
                          │    S    │      ♣ A 7 5
                          └─────────┘
```

Dealer South
Neither vul.

WEST	NORTH	EAST	SOUTH
			1♠
pass	4♣	pass	4♠
all pass			

North's 4♣ bid was described as a variation of Swiss, showing a good raise to 4♠. South's 4♠ meant that he was not interested in a slam. Nowadays most good players would reserve the response of 4♣ for a hand with a singleton or void in clubs and use either 2NT or 3NT as the way to show a raise with no short suit.

West led the ♣8, and Trick 1 went small, ace, and queen. East-West were playing 'second and fourth leads': leading fourth highest from a long suit headed by the ten or better and second highest from a collection of small cards.

What should East lead to the next trick?

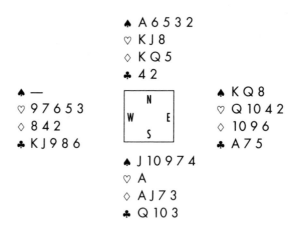

```
              ♠ A 6 5 3 2
              ♡ K J 8
              ◇ K Q 5
              ♣ 4 2
♠ —                             ♠ K Q 8
♡ 9 7 6 5 3      N              ♡ Q 10 4 2
◇ 8 4 2       W     E           ◇ 10 9 6
♣ K J 9 8 6      S              ♣ A 7 5
              ♠ J 10 9 7 4
              ♡ A
              ◇ A J 7 3
              ♣ Q 10 3
```

West led the eight of clubs. East won with the ace and South dropped a deceptive queen.

Believing that his partner had led second highest from a holding such as ♣9-8-6-3, East returned a heart, aiming to score two aces and two trump tricks. Sadly for East, when the declarer discovered the trump position, he was able to play four rounds of diamonds, discarding the second club from dummy, and so make his contract.

'I put South with the high clubs,' East explained to his partner. 'I was worried that, not knowing I had two trump tricks, you might have ducked a heart lead and lost your ace.'

'I wouldn't have been so foolish,' West replied. 'Suppose I had held four small and you had returned the seven of clubs; then I would have guessed that South held ♣K-Q-J-10. I would also have worked out that he might discard two hearts from dummy on his clubs, so I wouldn't have let him slip through a heart to the king'.

East's heart switch was the kind of play that only a good player would consider, but if you think it through then the play can hardly be right.

Glimmer of Light

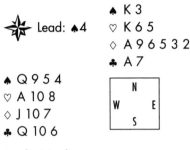

★ Lead: ♠4

♠ K 3
♡ K 6 5
◇ A 9 6 5 3 2
♣ A 7

♠ Q 9 5 4
♡ A 10 8
◇ J 10 7
♣ Q 10 6

Dealer North
Neither vul.

WEST	NORTH	EAST	SOUTH
	1◇	pass	1♡
pass	2◇	pass	2NT
pass	3NT	all pass	

North might (indeed probably should) have bid 3♡ over 2NT, offering his partner a choice of games, but perhaps he feared such a bid would be passed.

Sitting West, you lead a low spade to the ♠10 and South's ♠J. Declarer then leads a low diamond, the ◇8 to be precise. You go in with the ◇10 and are allowed to hold the trick, East playing the ◇4. How do you read the diamond position, and how do you continue?

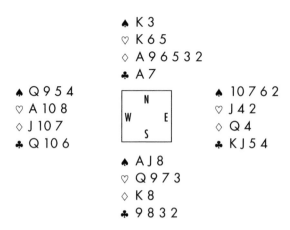

♠ K 3
♡ K 6 5
◇ A 9 6 5 3 2
♣ A 7

♠ Q 9 5 4
♡ A 10 8
◇ J 10 7
♣ Q 10 6

♠ 10 7 6 2
♡ J 4 2
◇ Q 4
♣ K J 5 4

♠ A J 8
♡ Q 9 7 3
◇ K 8
♣ 9 8 3 2

North-South have arrived in what you hope is a borderline 3NT. Your spade lead has run to the ten and jack. South then leads the eight of diamonds and allows your ten to win.

First, how do you suppose the diamonds lie? With ◇Q-x declarer would probably cross to dummy and hope to find East with the king. Most likely he holds ◇K-x. Either he wants to conceal his strength in the suit or he needs the king as an entry.

What about the spades? It is consistent with the play to the first trick for East to hold something like ♠A-10-x, but in this case he would surely overtake the diamond and lay down the ace. It seems far more likely South has ♠A-J-x or ♠A-J-x-x.

Now a glimmer of light is beginning to appear: the declarer expects you to play a second spade so that he can cross to the ◇K, cash his ♠A, and run nine tricks.

It looks as though his weakness is in clubs. Make life easy for partner: lead the ♣Q. With the spades blocked, South will be able to run only eight tricks: ♣A, back to the ◇K, spade to the king and four diamond winners. Even if he only cashes three diamonds, he will find discards from hand very awkward.

It is true that your opponent could have made the contract by cashing three spades early on, but that is not your concern.

Entry Plan

```
          ♠ K J 10 5
          ♡ A 8
          ◇ K Q 4
          ♣ Q J 10 2
                              ♠ A 4
              ┌───────┐       ♡ K Q 9 6 5
   Lead: ♡7   │   N   │       ◇ 9 7 2
              │ W   E │       ♣ K 7 4
              │   S   │
              └───────┘
```

Dealer East
Neither vul.

WEST	NORTH	EAST	SOUTH
		1♡	pass
2♡	dbl	pass	3◇
all pass			

In this sequence from an old match, you cannot readily tell whether South has a bust or almost enough to look for game. In modern competition play, some pairs use a 2NT bid by South as artificial, asking North to bid 3♣ so South can sign off; this would make South's direct 3◇ forward-going. The downside of the method is that South cannot bid a natural 2NT; he generally has to jump to 3NT or play for penalties.

West leads the ♡7, which runs to the ♡8, the ♡Q and the ♡10. You play five-card majors, so it looks like West has led his top card from three small (better than the middle card when his raise has told you that he cannot have a doubleton) and South has played an innocuous false card. How do you assess your chances? What do you lead to the next trick?

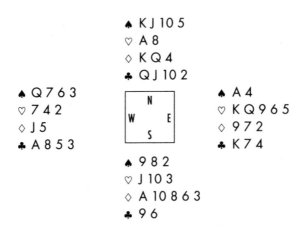

$\spadesuit$ K J 10 5
$\heartsuit$ A 8
$\diamond$ K Q 4
$\clubsuit$ Q J 10 2

$\spadesuit$ Q 7 6 3
$\heartsuit$ 7 4 2
$\diamond$ J 5
$\clubsuit$ A 8 5 3

$\spadesuit$ A 4
$\heartsuit$ K Q 9 6 5
$\diamond$ 9 7 2
$\clubsuit$ K 7 4

$\spadesuit$ 9 8 2
$\heartsuit$ J 10 3
$\diamond$ A 10 8 6 3
$\clubsuit$ 9 6

West leads the $\heartsuit$7, which runs to the queen, South dropping the ten.

It is clear that you must place partner with the $\clubsuit$A because otherwise it will prove impossible to find five tricks.

The original East laid down the $\clubsuit$K and then returned a heart. His idea was that declarer, placing him with both the top clubs, might misguess spades. Two thoughts occur: if you plan this type of strategy you may do better to win the first heart with the king; secondly, it hardly seems likely that your opponent will play spades before a second round of clubs.

A better plan, taking into account South's lack of entries, is to return the $\spadesuit$4. This is not a deceptive play but an entry move. Say that declarer wins with the ten in dummy and plays a club, which is as good as anything. You hop up with the king, cash the $\spadesuit$A, and play a club to West's ace. Now he gives you a ruff.

Declarer may, alternatively, draw trumps after your spade return. Then a second round of hearts will ensure two hearts, two clubs and a spade for the defenders. Only if declarer had put up the $\heartsuit$A on the first trick and gone after clubs could he have made nine tricks. Luckily for you, this line was not too obvious.

Do It Yourself

```
        ♠ J 9 8 7 4
        ♡ A K 10
        ◊ Q 3
        ♣ 8 6 2
                              ♠ A 6 3
  ✷ Lead: ◊J    ┌─────┐       ♡ 5 4
                │  N  │       ◊ K 8 6 5 2
                │W   E│       ♣ A 9 4
                │  S  │
                └─────┘
```

Dealer East
E–W vul.

WEST	NORTH	EAST	SOUTH
		pass	1♡
pass	1♠	pass	2♡
pass	3♡	pass	4♡
all pass			

Some players would open this East hand; point-count tends to undervalue aces and kings. However, you won't often miss game by passing and the suits do not have much stuffing.

West leads the ◊J and the ◊Q, ◊K and ◊A all cover this. Declarer crosses to the ♡K and leads the ♠9 from dummy. What plan do you form now?

Bear in mind that if your opponent has something like ♠K-10 then it may be a mistake to hesitate as you would then be more or less forced to play the ace. This is just a general remark, not a clue to the play on the present occasion.

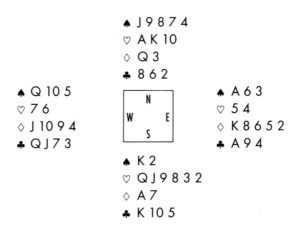

```
              ♠ J 9 8 7 4
              ♡ A K 10
              ◇ Q 3
              ♣ 8 6 2

♠ Q 10 5          N          ♠ A 6 3
♡ 7 6         W       E      ♡ 5 4
◇ J 10 9 4        S          ◇ K 8 6 5 2
♣ Q J 7 3                    ♣ A 9 4

              ♠ K 2
              ♡ Q J 9 8 3 2
              ◇ A 7
              ♣ K 10 5
```

West starts with the jack of diamonds; the queen, king and ace
cover this. After a heart to the king, declarer advances the nine of
spades from dummy.

This always creates an unpleasant situation for the defender
because he has to make up his mind at once whether to play the
ace or give declarer a chance to finesse when holding a ♠K-10
doubleton. Here you can make a good case for going up with the
ace because it might be a mistake to play low even when declarer
holds ♠K-x. Winning with the king, declarer would return a
spade and use the trump entries in dummy to establish the suit
with a ruff, losing just one spade, one diamond and one club.

Naturally, going up with the ♠A is not the end of the story.
After cashing the ♣A, you must then find the more difficult play
of returning your second heart, thereby removing a vital entry
from dummy before declarer can make use of it.

Admittedly, a diamond back followed by a trump from partner might produce the same result, but why put pressure on him?

Moderate Lead

                        ♠ A J 10 9
                        ♡ A K 6 3
                        ◇ 6
                        ♣ Q J 6 5

                                              ♠ 8 7 6 5 2
    Lead: ◇K   ♡ 10 8 2
                                              ◇ A 5
                                              ♣ 4 3 2

Dealer West
N–S vul.

WEST	NORTH	EAST	SOUTH
1◇	dbl	pass	1NT
pass	2◇	pass	2♠
pass	3♠	pass	4♠
all pass			

With five trumps and an ace facing partner's opening bid, and a less than convincing sequence, nobody would blame you for doubling. All the same, the small size of your trumps and the three-card holdings in the unbid suits forewarn of an opposing crossruff.

West leads the ◇K. As South responded 1NT on the first round it seems likely he has only three spades, and you may feel annoyed that partner has not led a trump. Still, you don't have to give up. What is your general plan?

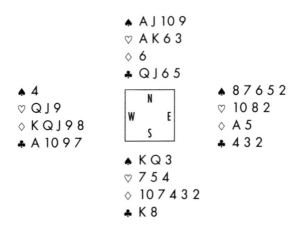

```
                      ♠ A J 10 9
                      ♡ A K 6 3
                      ◇ 6
                      ♣ Q J 6 5
  ♠ 4                                    ♠ 8 7 6 5 2
  ♡ Q J 9           ┌──────────┐         ♡ 10 8 2
  ◇ K Q J 9 8       │    N     │         ◇ A 5
  ♣ A 10 9 7        │ W      E │         ♣ 4 3 2
                    │    S     │
                    └──────────┘
                      ♠ K Q 3
                      ♡ 7 5 4
                      ◇ 10 7 4 3 2
                      ♣ K 8
```

West should no doubt lead a trump (generally correct when one opponent has a three-suited hand), but he begins instead with the king of diamonds.

It may seem natural to overtake and lead a trump. However, you achieve nothing much by this because you will not regain the lead to play another round of trumps. Declarer, in fact, will make game with six spade tricks (four in dummy and two by ruffing in hand), two hearts and two clubs (after knocking out the ace).

It is not very easy to see, perhaps, that the best line is to overtake the diamond and return the suit. The advantage of this is that when partner comes in with the ♣A he will be able to lead a third round of diamonds, on which you will discard a club. This deprives declarer of one of his top tricks and he cannot recover from this loss if you defend sensibly. In theory, of course, you could achieve the same result by leaving your partner on lead, but the situation may be less clear to him. He might, for example, think you want a trump switch.

Discarding losers so that you can ruff declarer's winners is a useful strategy to remember. Too many defenders rush to part with their 'useless' trumps in a dubious cause.

Among the Dead Men

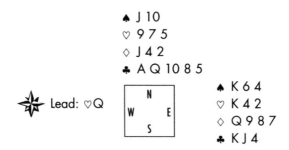

♠ J 10
♡ 9 7 5
◇ J 4 2
♣ A Q 10 8 5

Lead: ♡Q

♠ K 6 4
♡ K 4 2
◇ Q 9 8 7
♣ K J 4

Dealer South
Both vul.

WEST	NORTH	EAST	SOUTH
			1NT
pass	2NT	pass	3♠
pass	3NT	all pass	

South's 1NT shows 15-17 points and 2NT is invitational. As for the bid of 3♠, North explains that the partnership style is to open 1NT freely with a five-card major but that they play ordinary rather than five-card Stayman. Therefore, South's bid indicates a non-minimum with five spades and, presumably, a desire to play in 4♠ if North has three-card support and a ruffing value.

West leads the ♡Q and dummy plays low. How do you defend, both on the present trick and later?

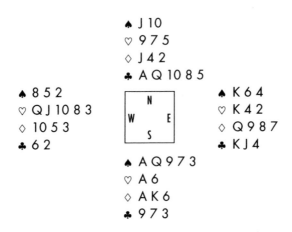

```
              ♠ J 10
              ♡ 9 7 5
              ◇ J 4 2
              ♣ A Q 10 8 5
♠ 8 5 2                           ♠ K 6 4
♡ Q J 10 8 3      N              ♡ K 4 2
◇ 10 5 3      W       E          ◇ Q 9 8 7
♣ 6 2             S              ♣ K J 4
              ♠ A Q 9 7 3
              ♡ A 6
              ◇ A K 6
              ♣ 9 7 3
```

West leads the queen of hearts against 3NT.

Since South has followed a sequence suggesting 16-17 points in his system, you can judge that there is scarcely room for West to hold anything more than the ♡Q-J. This being the case, you can count nine tricks for declarer: five spades, one heart, two diamonds and one club; this gives you permission to play some false cards. You should see at once that it might be a good plan to overtake the ♡Q with the ♡K and fire back the ♡2. This will at least cause declarer to misjudge the heart situation.

If declarer believes hearts are 6-2, he may finesse in clubs, thinking it gives him an extra chance; this would suit you fine. If not, then declarer will decide he needs to find East with the king of spades. A likely line for him then is to win the second heart and cross to the ♣A, intending to finesse in spades. Maintaining your usual calm exterior, you drop the ♣K under the ace. 'Oh well', says South to himself, 'I won't need the spade finesse. I can come back to hand with a diamond and pick up five tricks in clubs.' You come in with your ♣J and, somewhere among the dead men, you find the ♡4.

Unexpected Offer

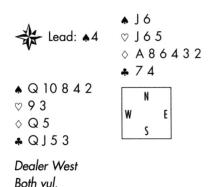

✿ Lead: ♠4

♠ J 6
♡ J 6 5
♢ A 8 6 4 3 2
♣ 7 4

♠ Q 10 8 4 2
♡ 9 3
♢ Q 5
♣ Q J 5 3

```
      N
  W       E
      S
```

Dealer West
Both vul.

WEST	NORTH	EAST	SOUTH
	pass	pass	2NT
pass	3NT	all pass	

As West, you lead the ♠4, which is covered by the ♠J and partner's king. East returns the ♠9. Declarer, with a learned air, wins with the ace and plays a third round, to which your partner follows as dummy throws a diamond.

What is going on with this play in the spade suit and what will you do now?

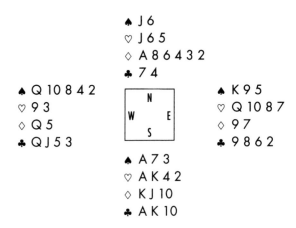

You lead the four of spades against 3NT and, surprisingly, declarer wins the second round and exits with a spade.

If, as West, you have not seen this kind of position before, you may think declarer has something like ◇K-x and wants to set up a squeeze of some sort. You may have decided to cash just one more spade and then switch to clubs.

This would backfire because South has a different plan in mind: cashing even one spade gives him a chance to unblock the diamonds by discarding the ◇10. The best strategy is to lead the ♣Q. Then, if declarer wins and tries the ◇10, you must be sure to cover with the queen.

These 'second hand high' situations can prove quite tricky unless you are ready for them. For example:

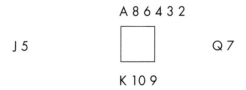

If dummy is short of entries and South leads the nine, you may need to cover with the jack. This is assuming, of course, that from declarer's point of view, yours is the danger hand.

<table>
<tr><td></td><td>♠ K 10 4</td></tr>
<tr><td></td><td>♡ K Q 9 2</td></tr>
<tr><td></td><td>◇ A 7 4</td></tr>
<tr><td></td><td>♣ K 6 4</td></tr>
</table>

♠ K 10 4
♡ K Q 9 2
◇ A 7 4
♣ K 6 4

Lead: ♠J

♠ A Q 8 6 3
♡ A 10
◇ K Q 9 5
♣ 9 2

Dealer North
E–W vul.

WEST	NORTH	EAST	SOUTH
	1NT	2♠	3♣
pass	3NT	pass	4♡
all pass			

North's 1NT is in the 14-16 range, making the East hand fractionally too weak to double for penalties. Your overcall of 2♠ conveys a deeper meaning than may first appear because you are playing a convention: you promise a minor suit as well, so that if your partner is short of spades he can inquire for the minor by bidding 2NT. The opponents describe South's 3♣ as constructive.

West leads the ♠J. The ♠K and the ♠A cover this, South dropping the ♠9. You must allow for the possibility (even the likelihood) that partner, leading through the notrump opener, will begin with a high spade whatever his length in the suit. How do you aim to defeat this contract?

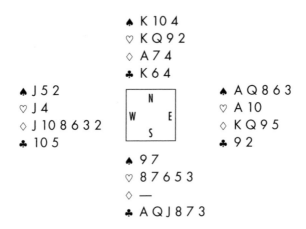

```
              ♠ K 10 4
              ♡ K Q 9 2
              ◇ A 7 4
              ♣ K 6 4
♠ J 5 2                         ♠ A Q 8 6 3
♡ J 4          ┌─────────┐     ♡ A 10
◇ J 10 8 6 3 2 │ W   N  E│     ◇ K Q 9 5
♣ 10 5         │     S   │     ♣ 9 2
              └─────────┘
              ♠ 9 7
              ♡ 8 7 6 5 3
              ◇ —
              ♣ A Q J 8 7 3
```

West leads the jack of spades through the notrump opener. You win with the ace and South drops the nine.

It is not difficult to gauge the distribution. South, who has introduced clubs at the three-level and hearts at the four-level, must be at least 5-6 in those suits. His ♠9, though a clever attempt at deception, seems suspect: West, with length in spades and diamonds, might well have entered the auction.

In any case, there is no better chance than to play queen and another spade, take the ♡K with the ace, and play a fourth spade. You hope partner can overruff declarer with the ♡J, promoting a trump trick whether or not dummy also overruffs.

On this deal South voluntarily introduced a weak suit. More typical examples of when declarer might turn up with a set of low trumps include: (a) if he makes a minimum response to his partner's takeout double; (b) if he merely completes a transfer; and (c) when he bids the suit as an artificial negative. In all three cases he could be vulnerable to an overruff and, in cases (a) and (c), he may have entry problems as well.

Good Recovery

```
            ♠ A 9 5 3
            ♡ 6 4
            ◇ 9 7 5
            ♣ K J 10 9
                                ♠ 8 4 2
  Lead: ◇K    ┌───────┐        ♡ K Q J 7 2
             │   N   │        ◇ A
             │ W   E │        ♣ A 8 7 4
             │   S   │
             └───────┘
```

Dealer South
N–S vul.

WEST	NORTH	EAST	SOUTH
			1♠
3◇	3♠	all pass	

East-West were playing weak jump overcalls when they were not vulnerable. East, not a supporter of the method but perhaps an advocate of the Law of Total Tricks, thought to himself, 'I dare not risk bidding at the four-level but when they go to 4♠, I'll chance a double.' The chance never came. East, over 3♠, was slow-witted. He should have bid 4◇: it looks safe on his values and might have persuaded an opponent with three small diamonds to bid 4♠ (expecting his partner to be short of diamonds).

When West led the ◇K against 3♠, East recovered to the extent that he defended well. What do you think he did?

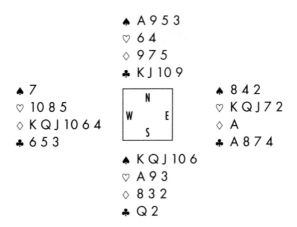

```
                 ♠ A 9 5 3
                 ♡ 6 4
                 ◇ 9 7 5
                 ♣ K J 10 9
♠ 7                              ♠ 8 4 2
♡ 10 8 5          N              ♡ K Q J 7 2
◇ K Q J 10 6 4   W   E           ◇ A
♣ 6 5 3           S              ♣ A 8 7 4
                 ♠ K Q J 10 6
                 ♡ A 9 3
                 ◇ 8 3 2
                 ♣ Q 2
```

Defending against 3♠, West leads the king of diamonds, which is overtaken by the ace.

If East had defended unimaginatively, for example by switching to a high heart, South would have ducked and easily made an overtrick by way of five top spades, the ♡A and a heart ruff, and three tricks in clubs. However, the original East had the wit to switch to a low heart. Now the contract could not be made. Even if declarer had gone up with the ace and drawn trumps, there would still have been an entry to the West hand.

What would have happened if South had held ♡A-10-x instead? At worst, he would have been presented with an extra overtrick and, at best, he might have failed to insert the ten.

With a holding like A-K-Q or K-Q-J, you usually lead high to avoid giving away a cheap trick. When, as above, you badly need to find a way to partner's hand, you should think nothing of leading low instead. If you have a void somewhere, you might do this even on the opening lead.

Special Messenger

```
                    ♠ A 5 4
                    ♡ J 10 8 5
                    ◇ Q 10 3
                    ♣ K Q 6
                              ♠ 8 4 2
            Lead: ◇K    N     ♡ 7
                      W   E   ◇ 9 7 5 2
                        S     ♣ A 8 7 5 3
```

Dealer East
E–W vul.

WEST	NORTH	EAST	SOUTH
		pass	1♡
pass	3♡	pass	4♡
all pass			

West leads the ◇K. You play the ◇7 and South the ◇J. West shifts to the ♣9 and dummy plays low.

There is a bit of a mystery about the whole affair because East-West normally lead the ace from A-K. This general method has something to commend it since if the lead of the king might be from ace-king or king-queen, leader's partner does not know whether to encourage with a doubleton (good in a suit contract opposite ace-king but not king-queen) or with jack and others (useful facing king-queen but not ace-king). Some pairs seek to get around this by playing a count signal on the king and an attitude signal on the ace, though then the opening leader has to predetermine what kind of signal he wants.

Sitting East, how do you assess what is happening? Has your partner fallen asleep? How do you play at this point?

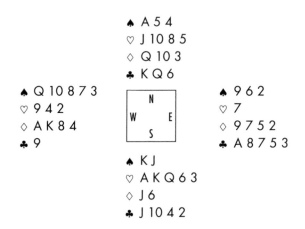

♠ A 5 4
♡ J 10 8 5
◇ Q 10 3
♣ K Q 6

♠ Q 10 8 7 3
♡ 9 4 2
◇ A K 8 4
♣ 9

♠ 9 6 2
♡ 7
◇ 9 7 5 2
♣ A 8 7 5 3

♠ K J
♡ A K Q 6 3
◇ J 6
♣ J 10 4 2

Against 4♡, West leads the king of diamonds. You play the seven to indicate an even number of cards in the suit, and South drops the jack. Now West switches to the nine of clubs.

The normal understanding between you and your partner is to lead the ace from an ace-king combination. Thus the king would be the correct card from a doubleton ◇A-K. If West does hold the doubleton, however, he would surely follow the king with the ace and when he does not, you may be confused.

The explanation is that the irregular card, in this case the king from a combination including the ace, king and others, has a 'sit up and take notice' meaning. West plays this card because he wants you to know the ♣9 is a singleton. Knowing this, you can put up the ace and give him a ruff. The message proves useful here as otherwise you might hold up on the first round of clubs, reading partner for a doubleton club and something like ♡K-x-x.

Derek Rimington introduced the idea of leading the king before switching to a singleton in a BOLS tip; in certain circles, this has since become known as an 'alarm clock' lead.

Awkward Moment

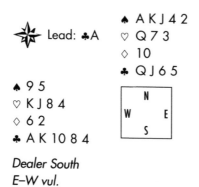

Lead: ♣A

♠ A K J 4 2
♡ Q 7 3
♢ 10
♣ Q J 6 5

♠ 9 5
♡ K J 8 4
♢ 6 2
♣ A K 10 8 4

```
      N
  W       E
      S
```

Dealer South
E–W vul.

WEST	NORTH	EAST	SOUTH
			1◇
pass	1♠	pass	2◇
pass	3♣	pass	3NT
all pass			

If you had been sitting East, you would have been able to make a takeout double after 1◇–pass–1♠. As it was, if not for the vulnerability, you might have doubled 2◇. You feel glad about keeping quiet when your opponents sail into game.

You have an awkward choice of lead. Any suit other than diamonds might be right. Eventually you decide on the ♣A. At least you will stay in command and the choice of lead at the next trick may prove easier.

Your ace draws the ♣3 from partner and the ♣7 from declarer. Your worries are not over. What do you try next?

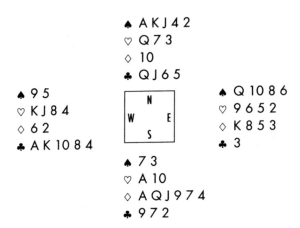

```
                    ♠ A K J 4 2
                    ♡ Q 7 3
                    ◊ 10
                    ♣ Q J 6 5
    ♠ 9 5              ┌─────────┐      ♠ Q 10 8 6
    ♡ K J 8 4          │    N    │      ♡ 9 6 5 2
    ◊ 6 2            W │         │ E     ◊ K 8 5 3
    ♣ A K 10 8 4       │    S    │      ♣ 3
                       └─────────┘
                    ♠ 7 3
                    ♡ A 10
                    ◊ A Q J 9 7 4
                    ♣ 9 7 2
```

As West, you lead the ace of clubs: three from partner, seven from South.

There is no certainty how the whole play will turn out, but you must attempt to remove South's entry by switching to the ♡K. Even if South has ♡A-10-x he will have to let the king hold, unless his diamonds are solid. The best he can do as the cards lie is to win with the ace, lead a club to the jack, and overtake the ◊10 with the ◊J. Meanwhile, your partner will have played the ♡6 on your king, so when you come in with the ♣K you can safely lead the ♡J. East must exercise a degree of care with his discards on the clubs to avoid an endplay, but one way or another South will likely end up with eight tricks but not nine.

The tactic of attacking the sole entry to a long suit in dummy is well known (and it even has a name — the Merrimac Coup), yet some players are apt to have a blind spot when they come across a similar situation with the long suit concealed. Don't be one of them!

Nervous Wait

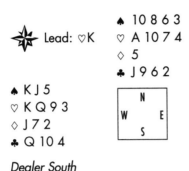

♦ 10 8 6 3
♡ A 10 7 4
◇ 5
♣ J 9 6 2

Lead: ♡K

♠ K J 5
♡ K Q 9 3
◇ J 7 2
♣ Q 10 4

N
W   E
S

Dealer South
Neither vul.

WEST	NORTH	EAST	SOUTH
			1◇
pass	1♡	pass	2♠
pass	3♠	pass	4♠
all pass			

North-South are playing Precision in which it is normal to open 1♣ with upwards of 16 points. Five-card majors are part of the system, making a 1◇ opening something of a moveable feast. However, South's jump shift promises real diamonds as well as a maximum 11-15 HCP hand.

You lead the ♡K and dummy's ace wins; ♡8 from partner (probably a count signal in this situation), ♡6 from South. Now declarer leads a low spade to the four, queen and king.

Your opening lead was not an easy choice and you have to play again, with the feeling that this may prove critical. What will you play?

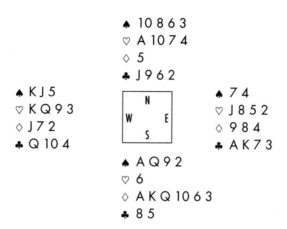

```
                    ♠ 10 8 6 3
                    ♡ A 10 7 4
                    ◇ 5
                    ♣ J 9 6 2
  ♠ K J 5            ┌─────────┐        ♠ 7 4
  ♡ K Q 9 3         │    N    │        ♡ J 8 5 2
  ◇ J 7 2           │ W     E │        ◇ 9 8 4
  ♣ Q 10 4          │    S    │        ♣ A K 7 3
                    └─────────┘
                    ♠ A Q 9 2
                    ♡ 6
                    ◇ A K Q 10 6 3
                    ♣ 8 5
```

Your lead of the king of hearts goes to dummy's ace and declarer leads a low spade to the queen and king.

You may have formed the impression from the play to the first trick that South has a singleton heart and that you can safely continue the suit. In this case you will sustain an unpleasant shock. Declarer will ruff, lay down the ♠A, and play on diamonds, discarding three clubs from dummy by the time you can get in with your master trump.

You must appreciate that South's bidding is most unusual for Precision — any opening bid other than 1♣ limits his high cards. The only plausible explanation is that he holds a strong diamond suit. His apparent disinterest in taking diamond ruffs confirms this. (He cannot afford to do so on his actual hand because he needs quick discards from dummy.)

When you win with the ♠K, you must attack clubs immediately. The queen is best; you don't want to lead the ♣4 to the king and sit there nervously waiting for partner to decide whether to return a club or a heart.

Overweight

```
           ♠ K 10 2
           ♡ A 9 7
           ◇ A K 8 6
           ♣ A K 2
                          ♠ A 9 5
              ┌─────┐     ♡ K Q 8 4 3
    Lead: ◇Q  │  N  │     ◇ 7
              │ W E │     ♣ Q 9 6 5
              │  S  │
              └─────┘
```

Dealer West
E–W vul.

WEST	NORTH	EAST	SOUTH
pass	2NT	pass	3♡
pass	4♣	pass	4♠
all pass			

South's 3♡ was a transfer bid, showing at least five spades, and North's 4♣ was a slam suggestion. Without any tenaces to protect, North does not mind too much the fact that this causes the strong hand to be on the table, and he does have an exceptional number of controls for a 2NT opening.

West leads the ◇Q. Declarer wins in dummy, leads a low spade to the queen, and returns a spade; this goes to the jack, king and ace.

The play often proves awkward for a defender who holds a high proportion of the outstanding strength. As East, what should you do now?

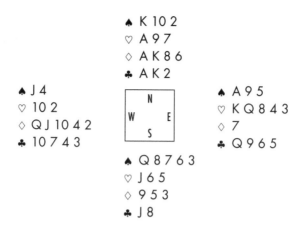

West leads the queen of diamonds against 4♠ and dummy's king wins. A low spade goes to the queen and declarer returns a spade to the jack, king and ace.

You count declarer for nine tricks — four spades and the five side winners in dummy. Unless West's diamonds are as good as ◇Q-J-10-9, a slow diamond winner will provide a tenth. This makes trying for two heart tricks the best chance. Switch to a low one, hoping West has ♡J-x or similar. Even if South has the ♡J, he may well not play it. If the ♡10 is allowed to hold, West must revert to the ◇J. East will ruff and the defenders will come to another trick.

Would you like to see another layout in which a defender does best to lead low rather than the higher of touching cards?

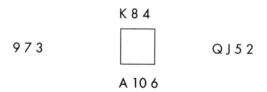

If East leads the two, declarer is unlikely to insert the ten, since this would lose if East had led from the Q-9 or J-9.

Small Deception

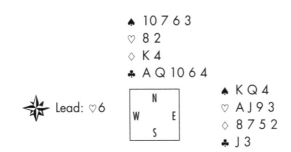

♠ 10 7 6 3
♡ 8 2
◇ K 4
♣ A Q 10 6 4

Lead: ♡6

```
        N
   W        E
        S
```

♠ K Q 4
♡ A J 9 3
◇ 8 7 5 2
♣ J 3

Dealer South
Both vul.

WEST	NORTH	EAST	SOUTH
			1♠
pass	2♣	pass	2◇
pass	3♠[1]	pass	4♠
all pass			

1. Invitational.

West leads the ♡6, you go up with your ♡A and declarer drops the ♡K.

On the bidding, you expected to find only three trumps in dummy (you guess that North responded 2♣ because he couldn't make up his mind whether to raise to 3♠ or 4♠) and prospects of defeating 4♠ do not look too good. Can you see any way of improving them?

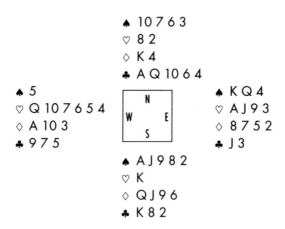

```
              ♠ 10 7 6 3
              ♡ 8 2
              ◊ K 4
              ♣ A Q 10 6 4
♠ 5                              ♠ K Q 4
♡ Q 10 7 6 5 4      N            ♡ A J 9 3
◊ A 10 3      W        E         ◊ 8 7 5 2
♣ 9 7 5              S           ♣ J 3
              ♠ A J 9 8 2
              ♡ K
              ◊ Q J 9 6
              ♣ K 8 2
```

A heart lead to your ace drops declarer's king.

Where will four tricks come from? You have scored a heart already and you must hope that your side can make a trick in one of the minors. This means you need two trump tricks, but the problem there is that holding something like ♠A-J-9-x-x declarer will probably take two finesses. (This is normally the correct play because it loses only when West holds a doubleton ♠K-Q and wins against either the singleton king or queen.)

When you win with the ♡A, the best move is to return the ♣J. If your opponent reads this card as a singleton, he will play the spades from the top — and perhaps partner will supply a trick in diamonds.

You need not worry unduly about finding West with a single-ton ♠J and ♣K-x-x. In that case, declarer could always succeed on a heart return by going on to duck a trump (better than cashing the ace), finessing the ♣Q, and cashing his top winners. A trump exit would then force you to furnish a ruff and discard; you still wouldn't get a club trick.

Fast Work

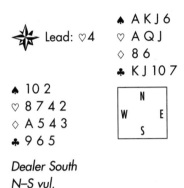

Lead: ♡4

♠ A K J 6
♡ A Q J
♢ 8 6
♣ K J 10 7

♠ 10 2
♡ 8 7 4 2
♢ A 5 4 3
♣ 9 6 5

```
    N
W       E
    S
```

Dealer South
N–S vul.

WEST	NORTH	EAST	SOUTH
			1NT
pass	2♣	pass	2♡
pass	3♠	pass	3NT
pass	6NT	all pass	

In the style of Precision that North-South play, they open 1♢ on minimum balanced hands and the 1NT opening shows 14-16. North's 2♣ asked for four-card majors. If North had only wished to play in game he would have bid 3NT over 2♡, expecting South to convert to 4♠ with 4-4 in the majors. On his actual hand, he had to improvise to make sure that any spade fit would come to light.

You make the neutral lead of a middle heart, won by dummy's queen. Barely pausing for breath, declarer leads a low diamond and puts up the king.

Have you decided what to do?

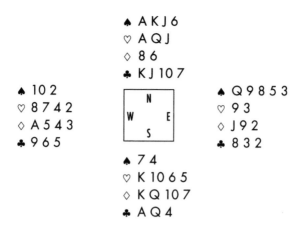

```
                    ♠ A K J 6
                    ♡ A Q J
                    ◊ 8 6
                    ♣ K J 10 7
    ♠ 10 2              ┌─────────┐        ♠ Q 9 8 5 3
    ♡ 8 7 4 2           │    N    │        ♡ 9 3
    ◊ A 5 4 3         W │       E │        ◊ J 9 2
    ♣ 9 6 5             │    S    │        ♣ 8 3 2
                        └─────────┘
                    ♠ 7 4
                    ♡ K 10 6 5
                    ◊ K Q 10 7
                    ♣ A Q 4
```

To give nothing away against 6NT, you begin with a heart. Declarer wins in dummy and leads a low diamond to the king.

The solution to this problem depends on timing rather than technique. Anyone could work out the right play, given time, but unless you put your brain into gear the moment dummy appears, you won't prove an effective opponent in this type of position.

Is there any possibility South has led a low diamond towards a holding like ◊K-10-x-x or ◊K-J-x-x? Not really, because if partner's maximum of 3 points included 2 or 3 in diamonds, declarer would have twelve top tricks — A-K-Q-J in each of the other three suits. This makes it right to duck the diamond as smoothly as you can. When he plays the next round of diamonds, your opponent will face a difficult decision because East, with ◊A-9-x, would again play low.

Note that with a slightly different hand it might prove effective for declarer to make an early lead of a low card towards an unsupported king. If the defender sitting over the king holds the ace but not the queen, it will often be a good play to duck.

Enterprise

♠ J 6 3
♡ 7 5
◇ 8 4 2
♣ A Q 6 5 2

♠ Q 10 8 4
♡ 8 6 2
◇ A 7 3
♣ 7 4 3

Lead: ◇J

N
W   E
S

Dealer North
N–S vul.

WEST	NORTH	EAST	SOUTH
	pass	pass	2♡
3◇	pass	4◇	4♡
pass	5♣	pass	6♡
all pass			

South has opened with an Acol two-bid (8+ playing tricks, natural and forcing for one round) and everyone has bid energetically. From the way the bidding has progressed, you suspect that someone playing weak twos would have opened the South hand 2♣, but in your opponents' system that would promise five quick tricks; for example, ace-king in two suits and ace in a third.

West leads the ◇J, you win with the ◇A and South drops the ◇Q. What do you play now?

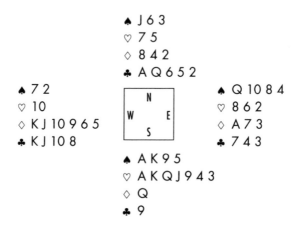

```
                    ♠ J 6 3
                    ♡ 7 5
                    ◇ 8 4 2
                    ♣ A Q 6 5 2
   ♠ 7 2              ┌───────┐        ♠ Q 10 8 4
   ♡ 10               │   N   │        ♡ 8 6 2
   ◇ K J 10 9 6 5     │ W   E │        ◇ A 7 3
   ♣ K J 10 8         │   S   │        ♣ 7 4 3
                      └───────┘
                    ♠ A K 9 5
                    ♡ A K Q J 9 4 3
                    ◇ Q
                    ♣ 9
```

West leads the jack of diamonds to your ace and South drops the queen.

It should not be too hard to see the danger of defending passively. If you play back a diamond, for instance, dummy's ◇8 will serve as a menace against West while the ♠9 acts as a menace against you. This leaves neither defender in a position to protect the third round of clubs when declarer runs the hearts.

The only real hope lies in playing South for a singleton club. Switch to a club, to break up the entries for a squeeze. In case South has a doubleton club, the club return does no harm, and he can hardly be void in clubs because North's bid of 5♣ drove him into the slam; besides, with 6-5 in the minors, West would probably have overcalled with an unusual 2NT.

After your club return, hoping to drop a doubleton ♠Q represents declarer's best bet. If instead he leads the ♠J from dummy in an attempt to pin the ♠10, you will cover with the ♠Q and he will be stuck in his own hand.

Too Keen

Lead: ♣A

North
♠ A 5
♡ 8 2
◇ A K Q 9 5 2
♣ 9 6 5

West
♠ K 9 8 3
♡ J 6 4
◇ 8
♣ A Q 10 7 3

```
      N
  W       E
      S
```

Dealer East
N–S vul.

WEST	NORTH	EAST	SOUTH
		pass	4♡
pass	6♡	pass	all pass

North's direct raise to 6♡ will not commend itself to scientific players, but there is much to be said for it. South is second in hand, vulnerable against not, and must hold good values. Also, opponents don't always lead the danger suit — unless, of course, you tell them all about it.

Sitting West, you face a difficult choice of opening lead. A trump lead, though probably safe, surrenders the initiative — not something you wish to do after this type of sequence. You decide to lead the ♣A; this collects the ♣4 from partner and the ♣K from South. At any rate, your lead has not proved fatal. How will you follow it up?

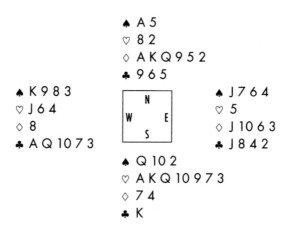

Defending against 6♡, you begin with the ace of clubs and the king falls from South. What do you try next?

Did you, by any chance, think of playing the ♠K? You would be making sure of knocking out the entry to the long diamonds in case declarer needs to ruff one round to set up the suit.

As you can see from the diagram, the ♠K won't strike a dangerous blow. Declarer will have tricks to spare.

How about switching to the ♠9? Expecting the diamonds to run, your opponent will surely put up dummy's ace. Then he will run the trumps but no squeeze develops.

Can you see another reason why the ♠K might backfire? If South held ♠J-x-x, for example, instead of ♠Q-x-x, you would be laying your partner open to a squeeze in spades and diamonds. Having gobbled up the ♠K with the ace, declarer would run all the trumps, reducing everyone to four cards. He would have two diamonds and the ♠J-x in hand, and four diamonds in dummy; East would be unable to keep four diamonds and the ♠Q.

Deeper Motive

```
            ♠ K J 9
            ♡ 7 4 2
            ◇ K 6 5
            ♣ A 10 7 4
                              ♠ 8 4 3
          Lead: ♠2    N       ♡ Q 10 6
                   W     E     ◇ Q 10 7 2
                      S        ♣ Q 9 6
```

Dealer South
Both vul.

WEST	NORTH	EAST	SOUTH
			1♠
pass	2♣	pass	2NT
pass	3♠	pass	4♠
all pass			

South's 2NT rebid is in the old-fashioned Acol style, with a range of 15-16.

It is not particularly important, but do you agree with North's 3♠ (rather than 3NT)? *The Bridge World* debated this point some years ago and reached the general conclusion that it was right to give partner a choice between 4♠ and 3NT. Interestingly, recent computer simulations have indicated that a completely flat hand (like North's) facing a 5332 type often fails to produce an extra trick when played in the suit. *The Bridge World* experts might take a different view if asked again today.

West leads a trump and dummy's ♠9 holds the trick. Declarer leads a low diamond from dummy. It's a bit odd, but you give count with the ◇7 and ... what happens?

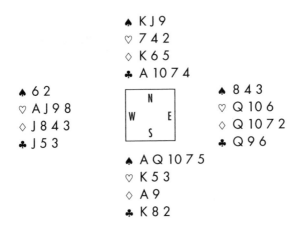

```
              ♠ K J 9
              ♡ 7 4 2
              ◇ K 6 5
              ♣ A 10 7 4
♠ 6 2                          ♠ 8 4 3
♡ A J 9 8        N             ♡ Q 10 6
◇ J 8 4 3     W     E          ◇ Q 10 7 2
♣ J 5 3          S             ♣ Q 9 6
              ♠ A Q 10 7 5
              ♡ K 5 3
              ◇ A 9
              ♣ K 8 2
```

West leads a trump, dummy's nine winning. Declarer leads a low diamond from dummy. It's a bit odd, but you follow with the seven and… what happens?

You find you have just given away the contract! Declarer will insert the ◇9, discard a club later on the king, and establish the thirteenth club for a heart discard.

The immediate lead of a low diamond off dummy certainly looked odd and you should have paused to consider what might be happening. Having considered, you insert the ◇10.

After winning with the ◇A, declarer may draw trumps ending on the table and call for a low club. Then you must stick in the ♣9 to prevent the trick from being ducked to partner. Soon enough you will get in with a club and be able to inflict the final blow by leading the ♡10 (or the ♡Q).

You won't find yourself caught out in situations like this if you make a habit of trying to figure out what declarer is trying to do. Although he might play on an unexpected suit simply to cross from one hand to the other to take a finesse, you should always stay alert to the possibility of a deeper motive.

Nothing Extra

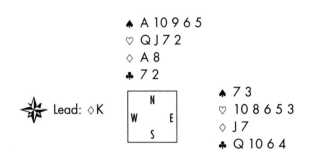

♠ A 10 9 6 5
♡ Q J 7 2
◇ A 8
♣ 7 2

Lead: ◇K

♠ 7 3
♡ 10 8 6 5 3
◇ J 7
♣ Q 10 6 4

Dealer South
Both vul.

WEST	NORTH	EAST	SOUTH
			1♠
2◇	4◇	pass	4NT
pass	5♣	pass	6♠
all pass			

In this somewhat antiquated bidding sequence, North's 4◇ indicated good support for spades but denied a singleton or the trump king. 4NT asked for additional features (side kings or the trump queen) and attracted a response in the negative. In case it affects how you view the situation, we must also point out that if West had overcalled 3◇, this would have shown a strong hand; he did not have a weak jump overcall available.

West leads the ◇K and dummy plays the ◇A. Sitting in the East seat, the only decision you can make at this point is whether to play the ◇J or the ◇7. It could prove important. Which do you choose, and why?

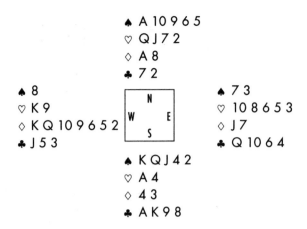

```
              ♠ A 10 9 6 5
              ♡ Q J 7 2
              ◇ A 8
              ♣ 7 2
♠ 8                              ♠ 7 3
♡ K 9                            ♡ 10 8 6 5 3
◇ K Q 10 9 6 5 2                 ◇ J 7
♣ J 5 3                          ♣ Q 10 6 4
              ♠ K Q J 4 2
              ♡ A 4
              ◇ 4 3
              ♣ A K 9 8
```

West led the king of diamonds and dummy's ace took this.

In a pairs event a fair proportion of the players in the East position dutifully recorded their doubleton by playing the ◇J. Can you see what that led to? Declarer drew trumps, eliminated the clubs, and exited with a diamond, which endplayed West.

'I had to show my doubleton', explained the East players. How could anyone be so foolish? You never have to show a doubleton or other distributional feature. Sometimes, in fact quite often, you must retain a possible entry card or guard.

Note that on this occasion no ethical problems arise if you are unable to play the ◇7 smoothly. If declarer strips the hand and leads a diamond towards the ◇8, it would make no sense for partner to go in with the ◇Q when he badly wants you to gain the lead and play a heart. However, as a rule, you should try to decide what you are going to play to the first trick while declarer studies the dummy. If, for example, dummy actually held ◇A-10 instead of ◇A-8, West might feel inconveniently placed in the end position.

Before He Knows

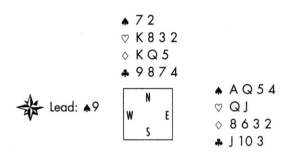

```
              ♠ 7 2
              ♡ K 8 3 2
              ◇ K Q 5
              ♣ 9 8 7 4
                              ♠ A Q 5 4
  Lead: ♠9     N             ♡ Q J
            W     E           ◇ 8 6 3 2
                S            ♣ J 10 3
```

Dealer North
N–S vul.

WEST	NORTH	EAST	SOUTH
	pass	pass	1♡
2♡	3♡	3♠	4♡
all pass			

West's 2♡ was a Ghestem variation, indicating (when he failed to compete further) a limited two-suiter with spades and diamonds. You are playing 'strong ten' leads, by which the ten would imply an interior sequence, so West's choice of the ♠9 shows a weak suit — probably ten high.

As East, you go up with the ♠A and South plays the ♠J. You can read the declarer for a doubleton ♠K-J and at most a singleton diamond. How do you propose to beat this contract?

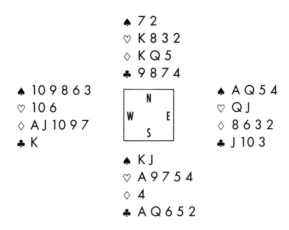

```
              ♠ 7 2
              ♡ K 8 3 2
              ◇ K Q 5
              ♣ 9 8 7 4
♠ 10 9 8 6 3              ♠ A Q 5 4
♡ 10 6        N          ♡ Q J
◇ A J 10 9 7  W    E     ◇ 8 6 3 2
♣ K              S       ♣ J 10 3
              ♠ K J
              ♡ A 9 7 5 4
              ◇ 4
              ♣ A Q 6 5 2
```

You win the first trick with the ace of spades and can read South for ♠K-J alone. What should you return?

You should consider the situation in this way: you can expect to make one trick in spades and one in diamonds. To beat the contract you will need two tricks in clubs. The correct play must be to attack this suit before declarer has been able to discover the distribution of the other suits.

You can see what will happen if you return a neutral card, say a spade. When declarer finds the trumps breaking 2-2 he will make the standard safety play in clubs, laying down the ace.

The position will look different if you simply switch to a low club. Declarer now has to guess whether West has a singleton heart or a singleton club. If he thinks the hearts are 3-1, he will reckon he cannot afford to lose any club tricks. In this case, he will finesse the ♣Q and later be chagrined to discover that he has gone down in a cold contract.

In Fashion

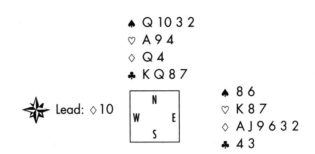

♠ Q 10 3 2
♡ A 9 4
◇ Q 4
♣ K Q 8 7

Lead: ◇ 10

♠ 8 6
♡ K 8 7
◇ A J 9 6 3 2
♣ 4 3

Dealer North
N–S vul.

WEST	NORTH	EAST	SOUTH
	1♣	2◇	3NT
all pass			

Weak jump overcalls are in fashion nowadays, especially in pairs events. Whether they materially improve the machinery of the defending side is another matter. Although you make your opponents' lives tougher in the auction (especially if partner can raise), the down side is that you make it easier for them to play the hand. A 1NT opening by North would have been strong, 15-17, hence his 1♣ bid.

West leads the ◇10 and the queen covers this. What plan do you form at this point?

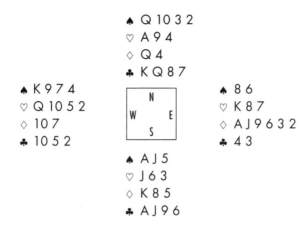

♠ Q 10 3 2
♡ A 9 4
◇ Q 4
♣ K Q 8 7

♠ K 9 7 4
♡ Q 10 5 2
◇ 10 7
♣ 10 5 2

♠ 8 6
♡ K 8 7
◇ A J 9 6 3 2
♣ 4 3

♠ A J 5
♡ J 6 3
◇ K 8 5
♣ A J 9 6

West leads the ten of diamonds and dummy plays the queen.

You definitely must win the trick to avoid giving declarer an extra winner and the only question now is whether to clear the suit or switch to hearts.

As South has jumped to 3NT, it seems unlikely that playing on diamonds will produce enough tricks in time. Your opponent will need to develop seven tricks in the black suits and this should not prove terribly difficult for him. (Six tricks in the blacks, followed by a throw-in may also suffice.)

In a pairs event the majority of defenders persevered with the diamonds. Declarer lost the spade finesse but came to nine tricks by way of three spades, one heart, one diamond and four clubs.

Although prospects do not appear very good, you should certainly try a switch to the ♡7. If North-South use negative doubles, declarer will rarely turn up with four hearts; even if he has the queen, he may not play it (although in that case you probably can't actually defeat the contract). As the cards lie, the low heart switch ensures five defensive tricks.

Future Expectation

```
              ♠ K J 10 8
              ♡ J 8 5
              ◇ Q 3 2
              ♣ Q J 10
                  ┌─────────┐         ♠ A Q 4
   ✳ Lead: ♡3     │    N    │         ♡ Q 9 2
                  │ W     E │         ◇ A 10 9 8
                  │    S    │         ♣ 9 6 2
                  └─────────┘
```

Dealer South
E–W vul.

WEST	NORTH	EAST	SOUTH
			1◇
pass	1♠	pass	1NT
pass	3NT	all pass	

South's rebid of 1NT, at this vulnerability, suggests 15-16. Within the constraints of the North-South system, South might have four clubs or four hearts or possibly both in a 1-4-4-4 shape. (Some play that you must always open 1♣ with 4-4 in the minors and others that you must start with 1◇. We belong to the third school — that you can open either one, normally going for the stronger suit. Our method works particularly well if partner ends up on lead or you have a slam on.)

West leads the ♡3 and dummy plays low. Even at this early stage, can you formulate a plan to defeat 3NT?

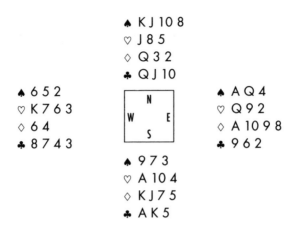

♠ K J 10 8
♡ J 8 5
◇ Q 3 2
♣ Q J 10

♠ 6 5 2
♡ K 7 6 3
◇ 6 4
♣ 8 7 4 3

♠ A Q 4
♡ Q 9 2
◇ A 10 9 8
♣ 9 6 2

♠ 9 7 3
♡ A 10 4
◇ K J 7 5
♣ A K 5

West begins with the three of hearts and dummy plays low.

Did you by any chance look at your cards and think, 'It's that old business of winning the first spade with the ace'?

Not so this time; indeed, wasting your ace would concede the contract. What you have to avoid is the 'automatic' finesse of the ♡9. Declarer will surely need to play on spades at some point, so you can see three certain winners in your hand. You should play the queen of hearts on the first trick. Declarer will win with the ace and take the spade finesse. After taking your queen, return the ♡9. Your partner, it is charitable to assume, will duck and so you will defeat the contract with two tricks in each major and one diamond.

If West has the ♡K, putting up the ♡Q succeeds if South's distribution is any of 3-3-4-3, 2-3-4-4, 2-3-5-3 or 1-3-5-4.

Could going up with the queen seriously backfire? It is true that if declarer has ♡A-K-x, you are giving him an easy trick; however, if you play the ♡9, the suit is frozen and you cannot beat the contract. Only if West has led from ♡K-10-x in preference to a four- or, more likely, five-card club suit, does it cost to play the queen. You must take that chance.

Early Concession

```
        ♠ K
        ♡ 7 5
        ◇ A K J 10 6 5 4
        ♣ 6 4 3
                          ♠ 8 6 4
  Lead: ♠5               ♡ 10 9 3
              N          ◇ Q 7 3
          W       E      ♣ K 10 7 5
              S
```

Dealer North
Neither vul.

WEST	NORTH	EAST	SOUTH
	1◇	pass	1♡
pass	2◇	pass	3NT
all pass			

West leads the ♠5 and dummy's king wins. You contribute the ♠4 and South the ♠10. You anticipate that the declarer will cash the ◇A or perhaps come to his hand to take the diamond finesse. In practice, he goes for an unexpected play — the ◇10 from dummy. You win with the ◇Q, all following. What do you do now?

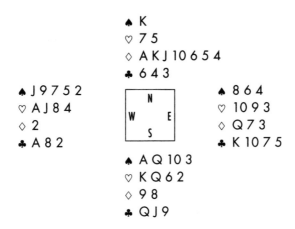

```
              ♠ K
              ♡ 7 5
              ◇ A K J 10 6 5 4
              ♣ 6 4 3
♠ J 9 7 5 2                    ♠ 8 6 4
♡ A J 8 4        N             ♡ 10 9 3
◇ 2          W       E         ◇ Q 7 3
♣ A 8 2          S             ♣ K 10 7 5
              ♠ A Q 10 3
              ♡ K Q 6 2
              ◇ 9 8
              ♣ Q J 9
```

West leads the five of spades, declarer playing a slightly decep-tive ten from hand. At the second trick, he leads the ten of dia-monds from dummy and you win with the queen.

It looks fairly clear what is happening. Declarer has ample guards everywhere and believes he can give up a diamond for safety while all the other suits remain under control. You can almost draw a diagram of his hand. In any case, the optimum strategy on such occasions is to cut your opponent adrift by returning the long suit, forcing him to run it immediately. You can keep three clubs and the discards for South will become increasingly embarrassing.

Note that even if the play had gone a bit differently, you would still have had reason to place South with strong spades. You would judge that West had around 10 points and at least a five-card spade suit; you might also know about his singleton diamond. When you added all this to the fact that West had the chance to overcall 1♠, non-vulnerable, yet failed to do so, you could deduce that his spades must be poor.

In Form

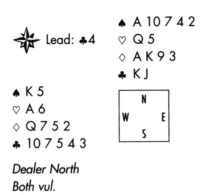

$\spadesuit$ Lead: $\clubsuit$4

$\spadesuit$ A 10 7 4 2
$\heartsuit$ Q 5
$\diamond$ A K 9 3
$\clubsuit$ K J

$\spadesuit$ K 5
$\heartsuit$ A 6
$\diamond$ Q 7 5 2
$\clubsuit$ 10 7 5 4 3

Dealer North
Both vul.

WEST	NORTH	EAST	SOUTH
	1$\spadesuit$	pass	1NT
pass	2$\diamond$	pass	2$\heartsuit$
pass	3$\heartsuit$	pass	4$\heartsuit$
all pass			

Some players would raise 1NT to 2NT in order to show their 17 points but 2$\diamond$ seems fine. If partner passes, it is unlikely that a game has been missed. Certainly North's raise to 3$\heartsuit$ looks well judged. His partner may well have a six-card suit and in this case 4$\heartsuit$ will probably be the best spot.

Sitting West, you lead the $\clubsuit$4 and are evidently in form for partner scores the $\clubsuit$Q and the $\clubsuit$A (South dropping the $\clubsuit$9 on the second round). After some thought partner shifts to the $\diamond$8. South plays the $\diamond$J and you decide not to cover. He continues with a low heart. What is your plan now?

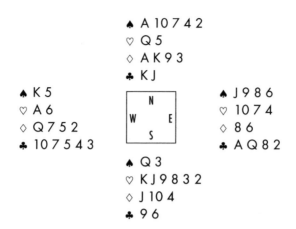

♠ A 10 7 4 2
♥ Q 5
♦ A K 9 3
♣ K J

♠ K 5
♥ A 6
♦ Q 7 5 2
♣ 10 7 5 4 3

♠ J 9 8 6
♥ 10 7 4
♦ 8 6
♣ A Q 8 2

♠ Q 3
♥ K J 9 8 3 2
♦ J 10 4
♣ 9 6

You lead a club against 4♡. Your partner takes the queen and ace, and then switches to the eight of diamonds. South plays the jack and you refrain from covering because you judge it unlikely that partner has led from ◇10-8. You have already formed your plan if he has ◇8-x.

Having scored the ◇J, declarer leads a small heart. You should play low. Dummy's queen wins and a second heart comes to your ace. Partner will probably play high-low in trumps to suggest a third trump and a desire for a ruff, although you know what to do anyway. You lead the ◇Q, leaving the declarer unhappily locked in dummy. You don't make a trick in spades but you have done enough with two clubs, one heart and a diamond ruff. You can give partner credit for his diamond shift — too many players only say something in the post mortem if they wish to complain — and nurturing partner is an important and neglected part of the game.

Choice of Three

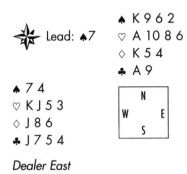

✿ Lead: ♠7

♠ K 9 6 2
♡ A 10 8 6
♢ K 5 4
♣ A 9

♠ 7 4
♡ K J 5 3
♢ J 8 6
♣ J 7 5 4

Dealer East
Neither vul.

WEST	NORTH	EAST	SOUTH
		pass	1NT[1]
pass	2♣	pass	2♡
pass	4♡	all pass	

1.   12-14.

South's 1NT is in the 12-14 range. In response to North's Stayman inquiry, South has shown four hearts (or maybe five — he wouldn't open 1♡ on ♡Q-9-x-x-x in a 5332 type; in fact, with a hand like that he probably wouldn't jump to 3♡ over 2♣ either, especially if minimum) and he has not denied four spades.

You lead the ♠7, which turns out quite well when East takes the ♠Q and the ♠A before playing a third round. After a little thought, declarer, who has so far followed with the ♠8 and the ♠J, ruffs with the ♡7.

He has given you a little time to think. Perhaps you didn't need it?

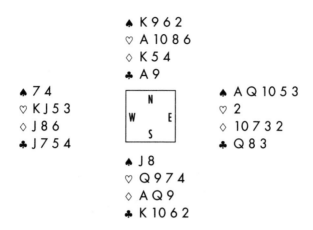

```
                    ♠ K 9 6 2
                    ♡ A 10 8 6
                    ◇ K 5 4
                    ♣ A 9
   ♠ 7 4                              ♠ A Q 10 5 3
   ♡ K J 5 3        ┌─────────┐       ♡ 2
   ◇ J 8 6          │    N    │       ◇ 10 7 3 2
   ♣ J 7 5 4        │ W     E │       ♣ Q 8 3
                    │    S    │
                    └─────────┘
                    ♠ J 8
                    ♡ Q 9 7 4
                    ◇ A Q 9
                    ♣ K 10 6 2
```

You lead the seven of spades against 4♡. Your partner makes the
queen and ace and plays a third round, South ruffing with the
♡7.

You have three possible plans now: (1) overruff with the jack;
(2) discard a diamond or club; (3) overruff with the king.

To overruff with the jack is weak: declarer has little choice
but to finesse you for the king, thereby making the contract easily.

To look the other way and discard from one of the minor suits
sounds more plausible; unfortunately, declarer may reflect that
East has already turned up with ♠A-Q-10-x-x. With this, the
♡K-J and possibly something in the minors, East might have
opened the bidding.

The best plan is to overruff with the ♡K. Declarer may have
come across this deceptive play before but there is still no convincing reason from his point of view why you should not hold
♡K-x and your partner ♡J-x-x. It seems likely — almost certain —
that when declarer comes in he will cash the ♡A rather than the
queen. He will then have to give up the setting trick to your ♡J.

Subtle Blow

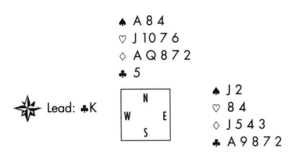

♠ A 8 4
♡ J 10 7 6
◇ A Q 8 7 2
♣ 5

Lead: ♣K

♠ J 2
♡ 8 4
◇ J 5 4 3
♣ A 9 8 7 2

Dealer North
E–W vul.

WEST	NORTH	EAST	SOUTH
	1◇	pass	1♡
dbl	2♡	3♣	3♡
4♣	4♡	all pass	

The North hand may not seem strong to those who reckon by points, but these 5431 types usually play well; also, North didn't know whether he could defeat your contract. Come to think of it, you wouldn't have bid 3♣ if you had valued your own hand solely in terms of points.

Your partner leads the ♣K. What is your plan?

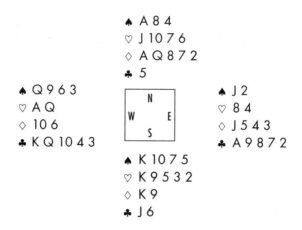

When partner leads the ♣K, prospects do not look good due to your side's wasted club values. The chance of a diamond trick seems slim, so you aim for two hearts and a spade, or two spades (perhaps via a ruff) and a heart.

In any case, you must overtake the ♣K with the ♣A and attack spades. Since you do not expect to regain the lead you must begin with a low spade — not the ♠J. It works! Declarer will play low from hand and capture the ♠9 with the ♠A. The ♡J runs to the queen and West can continue spades. Later partner will get back in to cash the setting trick in the suit.

Opportunities to lead low from a doubleton occur quite often:

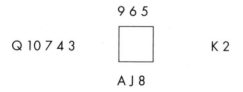

If East knows that West is the one with a later entry, he does best to attack this side suit by leading the two. It is true that declarer could block the suit by rising with the ace, but he is unlikely to do so.

Invitation to the Waltz

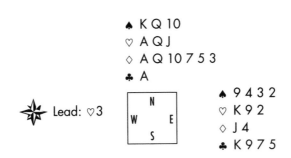

```
                    ♠ K Q 10
                    ♡ A Q J
                    ◇ A Q 10 7 5 3
                    ♣ A
                                      ♠ 9 4 3 2
            ❋ Lead: ♡3      N        ♡ K 9 2
                         W      E     ◇ J 4
                            S        ♣ K 9 7 5
```

Dealer North
Both vul.

WEST	NORTH	EAST	SOUTH
	2♣	pass	2◇
pass	3◇	pass	4◇
pass	4NT	pass	5◇
pass	6◇	all pass	

It is rubber bridge and North, sensing the rubber within his grasp,
opens 2♣, a strong and artificial bid, to which South gives a negative response. Later North applies the old Black and his side
soon reaches 6◇. North's attempt to play the contract is rejected
on all sides and West leads the ♡3. Declarer studies the dummy
for a minute or so (who would rush the play of the first trick in a
slam?) and calls for the queen from dummy.

Are you ready for a sparkling piece of defensive play?

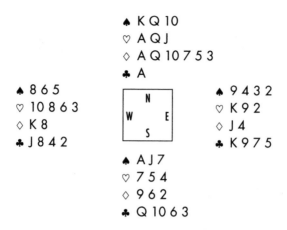

　　　　　♠ K Q 10
　　　　　♡ A Q J
　　　　　◇ A Q 10 7 5 3
　　　　　♣ A

♠ 8 6 5　　　　　　　　　　♠ 9 4 3 2
♡ 10 8 6 3　　　　　　　　♡ K 9 2
◇ K 8　　　　　　　　　　◇ J 4
♣ J 8 4 2　　　　　　　　♣ K 9 7 5

　　　　　♠ A J 7
　　　　　♡ 7 5 4
　　　　　◇ 9 6 2
　　　　　♣ Q 10 6 3

West leads the ♡3 against South's diamond slam and dummy plays the ♡Q.

While declarer took a little time to study the situation, you were able to reflect: 'South has the ace of spades but not, I imagine the king of diamonds, because one normally gives a positive response with an ace and a king. In any case, we have little hope if he has either the king of trumps or four small (South would have bid a six-card heart suit if he had one, so partner cannot ruff a heart return). If, however, he has only ◇9-x-x, can I persuade him to make the celebrated safety play in diamonds — ace first? Maybe, if he thinks that the heart finesse is right, he will do this.'

So you let the ♡Q hold. South, with a knowing air, elects to play the ◇A, come to hand with a spade and lead another trump. West wins and leads another heart but this time, to declarer's astonishment, the finesse doesn't work so well. Time to take a bow for the kibitzers!

What's He Up To?

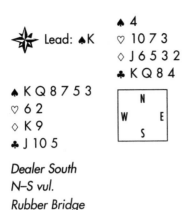

♠ 4
♡ 10 7 3
◊ J 6 5 3 2
♣ K Q 8 4

Lead: ♠K

♠ K Q 8 7 5 3
♡ 6 2
◊ K 9
♣ J 10 5

N
W   E
S

Dealer South
N–S vul.
Rubber Bridge

WEST	NORTH	EAST	SOUTH
			1♡
1♠	dbl	2♠	3♠
pass	4♡	all pass	

North's double is negative, implying in principle about 6-8 points. It strikes us as a questionable action even if South had only promised four hearts; with a weak hand and ruffing values, a raise to 2♡ must be better.

Notice you did not consider sacrificing in 4♠ (which would surely be doubled). At rubber bridge, if the opponents are already game up, they are halfway to winning the rubber, making the value of game only 350 (plus the trick score). The rubber setting may also explain why you did not have a weak jump overcall at your disposal.

You lead the ♠K, East plays the ♠J, and South wins with the ♠A. Now declarer leads the ◊7. What plan do you form at this point?

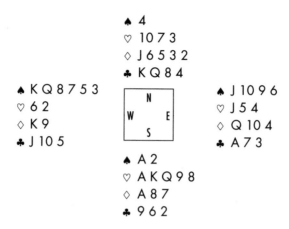

```
                    ♠ 4
                    ♡ 10 7 3
                    ◇ J 6 5 3 2
                    ♣ K Q 8 4
  ♠ K Q 8 7 5 3                          ♠ J 10 9 6
  ♡ 6 2            ┌──────────┐          ♡ J 5 4
  ◇ K 9           │     N    │          ◇ Q 10 4
  ♣ J 10 5        │  W     E │          ♣ A 7 3
                  │     S    │
                  └──────────┘
                    ♠ A 2
                    ♡ A K Q 9 8
                    ◇ A 8 7
                    ♣ 9 6 2
```

You lead the king of spades, East plays the jack (denoting a sequence headed by the jack) and the ace wins. Now declarer leads a low diamond.

This looks like one of those deals where you have to judge what your opponent is aiming to do. Most likely declarer holds ◇A-x-x and wishes to develop the suit for a club discard.

With any trump finesse working for declarer, you do not expect to make any trump tricks. The best plan is to try for two tricks in each minor. You should therefore take your ◇K and attack clubs by leading the ♣5. Even if declarer has the ♣9 and places East with the ace, he will not necessarily take the deep finesse. Suppose that he puts up the queen and that East wins and returns a club. After winning this trick in dummy, declarer will play a heart to the ace, ruff his spade loser and play off all the trumps, hoping for a squeeze if someone holds the master club and the guarded ◇Q.

Alternatively, East may allow the ♣Q to hold. Declarer may take a spade ruff and play off a few hearts, but defending the end position should prove easy enough.

Safe Return

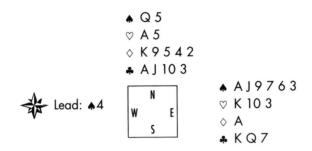

♠ Q 5
♡ A 5
◇ K 9 5 4 2
♣ A J 10 3

Lead: ♠4

♠ A J 9 7 6 3
♡ K 10 3
◇ A
♣ K Q 7

Dealer South
Both vul.

WEST	NORTH	EAST	SOUTH
			3◇
pass	5◇	dbl	all pass

You would double no matter whom you were playing, but you know South to be an undisciplined bidder, somebody who would think nothing of preempting on a six-card suit vulnerable or with a four-card major on the side. To bid 5♠ would be foolish indeed because partner would need to turn up with several useful cards to give you a play for eleven tricks; if he has them, you can surely extract a useful penalty.

West leads a low spade and when declarer ruffs the first trick North is pleased that he did not respond 3NT.

South begins by leading the ◇Q to your ace, West throwing a spade. You return a spade. After ruffing again, South leads a low club, which goes to the ♣6, the ♣J and the ♣K.

Now you have to find a good return. What do you suggest?

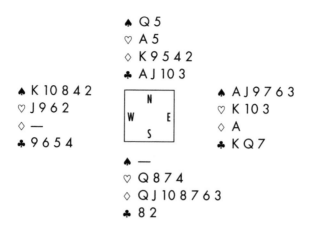

```
                    ♠ Q 5
                    ♡ A 5
                    ◇ K 9 5 4 2
                    ♣ A J 10 3
      ♠ K 10 8 4 2          N          ♠ A J 9 7 6 3
      ♡ J 9 6 2                         ♡ K 10 3
      ◇ —          W         E          ◇ A
      ♣ 9 6 5 4                 S       ♣ K Q 7
                    ♠ —
                    ♡ Q 8 7 4
                    ◇ Q J 10 8 7 6 3
                    ♣ 8 2
```

Having ruffed the spade lead, declarer plays a diamond to East's ace and ruffs the spade return. Then he leads a club to the jack and king.

You could make a song and dance about your next play but it boils down to this: South is known to hold six cards in hearts and clubs, so it must be safe to return a club and wait to score a heart trick. (Yes, one theoretical exception exists: if South has a 0-1-7-5 shape. However, it seems safe to assume that partner would have taken out the double on his 5-7-0-1!)

Here it is much better to lead into a tenace rather than concede a ruff and discard. On other occasions, if declarer has a 4-4 fit in a side suit, a single discard may not help him and the defenders do best to leave the suit well alone. This could be its layout:

```
              K 9 5 4
      10 3                A J 6
              Q 8 7 2
```

If West leads low or East leads high or low, they never make a second trick. If East leads the jack or West the ten, declarer should still succeed, by applying restricted choice principles.

Similar Type

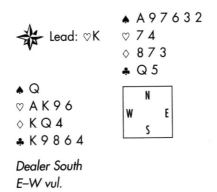

Lead: ♡K

```
            ♠ A 9 7 6 3 2
            ♡ 7 4
            ◇ 8 7 3
            ♣ Q 5
♠ Q
♡ A K 9 6        N
◇ K Q 4      W       E
♣ K 9 8 6 4      S
```

Dealer South
E–W vul.

WEST	NORTH	EAST	SOUTH
			1♠
dbl	4♠	all pass	

You were not far away from doubling again — perhaps the ◇A instead of the ◇K would have been enough. On your actual collection, with partner figuring to contribute little and a distinct danger that someone holds a singleton in one of the red suits, passing was eminently correct.

You lead the ♡K (or the ♡A), on which partner plays the ♡2 and declarer the ♡8. Not wanting to be on lead too often you lay down a second high heart, on which your partner plays the ♡5 and declarer the ♡Q. You exit with your spade. Dummy's ace wins, partner following suit, and declarer leads a diamond from the table, covered by the ◇2, the ◇J and your ◇K.

What do you play now? (Note that this problem resembles the previous one — but that can happen in real life too.)

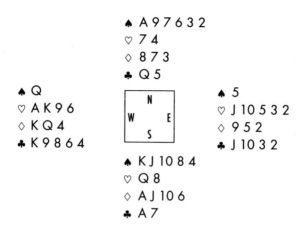

```
              ♠ A 9 7 6 3 2
              ♡ 7 4
              ◇ 8 7 3
              ♣ Q 5
♠ Q                         ♠ 5
♡ A K 9 6       N           ♡ J 10 5 3 2
◇ K Q 4    W        E       ◇ 9 5 2
♣ K 9 8 6 4     S           ♣ J 10 3 2
              ♠ K J 10 8 4
              ♡ Q 8
              ◇ A J 10 6
              ♣ A 7
```

Sitting West, you begin with the ace and king of hearts. (On the second round partner plays the five lest you interpret either the three or the jack as a suit-preference signal.) You switch to the queen of spades. Dummy's ace wins and declarer leads a diamond to the two, jack and king.

Based on the play so far, you can feel fairly confident that a heart would concede a ruff and discard, so you must surely choose between the minor suits. If your partner's ◇2 indicates an odd number of cards in the suit, South must have a 5-2-2-4 or 5-2-4-2 shape.

A strong pointer towards the latter is that with ♣A-10-x-x or ♣A-J-x-x, declarer might well have tried a low club towards the dummy and left you no winning option. If South is 5-2-4-2, a diamond back might let him score the ten and a long card, costing you two tricks; conversely, a club return appears safe even though it may concede a trick to the queen. It has to be right to return a club now.

And what if the club return proves disastrous, South holding ◇A-J bare and ♣A-7-3-2? In that case you can fall back on that old standby — blaming partner: 'With ◇10-9-6-5-2, why didn't you clarify the position by playing the ten instead of giving me a pointless length signal?'

Good Start

```
            ♠ A J 8 5 2
            ♡ J 8 3
            ◊ A Q 10
            ♣ K 3
                              ♠ K 9 3
         Lead: ◊6    N        ♡ A K Q 5
                 W       E     ◊ K J 8 7
                     S         ♣ 8 5
```

Dealer North
Both vul.

WEST	NORTH	EAST	SOUTH
	1♠	1NT	2♣
pass	pass	dbl	pass
2◊	pass	pass	3♣
all pass			

Since North-South were playing Precision, the 1♠ opening showed a five-card suit and a maximum of around 15 points. South's 2♣ was a fairly weak action; with a good hand, he would double. You would expect him to have a six-card suit to bid 2♣, and certainly when he bids the suit again — anybody going down when both sides are vulnerable is losing at least 100, so players are cautious about competing too much on a partscore deal.

West leads the ◊6 (second highest from weak suits), on which go the ◊10, the ◊J and the ◊3. You try a top heart and three rounds stand up, partner holding ♡10-x-x.

All seems to have gone well so far. What do you try next?

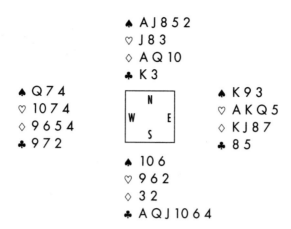

```
                    ♠ A J 8 5 2
                    ♡ J 8 3
                    ◇ A Q 10
                    ♣ K 3
  ♠ Q 7 4            ┌─────────┐        ♠ K 9 3
  ♡ 10 7 4          │    N    │        ♡ A K Q 5
  ◇ 9 6 5 4         │ W     E │        ◇ K J 8 7
  ♣ 9 7 2           │    S    │        ♣ 8 5
                    └─────────┘
                    ♠ 10 6
                    ♡ 9 6 2
                    ◇ 3 2
                    ♣ A Q J 10 6 4
```

West leads the six of diamonds, the ten loses to the jack, and you play off three top hearts, to which all follow. (Partner might have played his highest heart on the second round as suit-preference for spades if he held the queen, but you cannot rely on this.)

At this point a club looks dangerous because it might kill the queen in partner's hand. A fourth heart would allow a ruff and discard, and a low spade, as the cards lie, would force partner's queen and expose you to a squeeze in spades and diamonds. This makes your best continuation the ♠K. If South holds the queen, this return will not cost since in any event you would be squeezed in spades and diamonds.

There is one other faint possibility — that West has ♣Q-10 alone. In this case a fourth heart might lead to a trump trick. Having overruffed the ♣10 with dummy's king, declarer might finesse and lose to the now singleton queen. Dummy's play of the ◇10 on the first trick makes this unlikely; with only three cards in spades and diamonds, he would have played dummy's ◇Q or ◇A.

Finally, note that South would have done much better to defend against 1NT. You would have gone two down.

Right Moment

```
             ♠ 7 6 4 3
             ♡ J 9 3
             ◇ Q 9
             ♣ A K J 2
                              ♠ J 9 8 2
  Lead: ♠K         N          ♡ Q 10 7
              W        E       ◇ A 10 8 3
                   S           ♣ 8 6
```

Dealer South
N–S vul.

WEST	NORTH	EAST	SOUTH
			1♡
pass	3♡	pass	4♡
all pass			

Even though North-South are playing five-card majors, we don't think very much of North's 3♡ bid. Most good players reserve the jump raise for hands with four-card support since this helps opener to judge the later auction. (For example, he is much more likely to want to make a slam try or compete to the five-level facing known four-card support).

Partner leads the ♠K, you signal with the ♠9, and declarer wins with the ♠A. He cashes the ♡A and the ♡K, partner following suit, and turns his attention to clubs, leading queen and another. Partner plays the ♣3 and the ♣4. How do you play when dummy leads a third round of clubs?

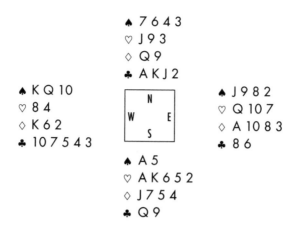

```
                    ♠ 7 6 4 3
                    ♡ J 9 3
                    ◇ Q 9
                    ♣ A K J 2
    ♠ K Q 10          ┌─────────┐      ♠ J 9 8 2
    ♡ 8 4             │    N    │      ♡ Q 10 7
    ◇ K 6 2          │ W     E │      ◇ A 10 8 3
    ♣ 10 7 5 4 3     │    S    │      ♣ 8 6
                     └─────────┘
                    ♠ A 5
                    ♡ A K 6 5 2
                    ◇ J 7 5 4
                    ♣ Q 9
```

Declarer, playing in 4♡, wins the lead of the ♠K with the ace.
After two rounds of trumps, he plays the queen and the nine of
clubs, followed by a third round of trumps.

You assume from the play that partner began with either
three clubs or five. If three, declarer will hold four and ruffing
with the master trump can serve little purpose. So, you consider
the situation in which West holds five clubs and South two.

One solid principle will save you from an error here: don't
ruff with a master trump when you have a chance to gain the lead
later and draw two trumps for one. If you ruff, South will discard
his losing spade and lose just two more tricks, ruffing one diamond and discarding the other. Let him throw a spade on the
third club and a diamond on the fourth. When you come in with
the ◇A (or the ◇10) you will draw dummy's trump and your side
will make one heart and three diamonds.

Declarer could have made the contract by cashing at most one
high trump before turning to clubs. He avoided this because he
was worried that someone would ruff a club with a doubleton
trump. He actually hoped the queen would fall in two rounds or,
in the alternative, that there would be a defensive error.

Logical Choice

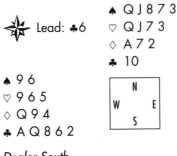

✦ Lead: ♣6

♠ Q J 8 7 3
♡ Q J 7 3
♢ A 7 2
♣ 10

♠ 9 6
♡ 9 6 5
♢ Q 9 4
♣ A Q 8 6 2

```
    N
W       E
    S
```

Dealer South
Neither vul.

WEST	NORTH	EAST	SOUTH
			1♢
pass	1♠	pass	2NT
pass	3♡	pass	3NT
all pass			

In the modern style, South's 2NT rebid showed 18-19. North's bid of 3♡ created a game force and, since he would have responded 1♡ with 4-4 in the majors, promised at least five spades and four hearts.

    You lead the ♣6 to the ♣10, the ♣7 (presumably showing four) and the ♣5. Now declarer leads the ♢2 from dummy, which goes six, jack, queen. You want to find an entry to partner in one of the majors. Which do you try, spades or hearts? Can you see a logical reason for your choice?

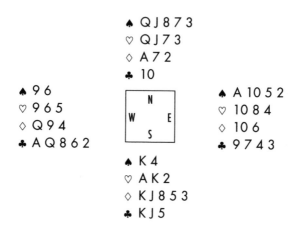

```
                    ♠ Q J 8 7 3
                    ♡ Q J 7 3
                    ◇ A 7 2
                    ♣ 10
  ♠ 9 6                              ♠ A 10 5 2
  ♡ 9 6 5              N             ♡ 10 8 4
  ◇ Q 9 4         W       E          ◇ 10 6
  ♣ A Q 8 6 2          S             ♣ 9 7 4 3
                    ♠ K 4
                    ♡ A K 2
                    ◇ K J 8 5 3
                    ♣ K J 5
```

You lead a low club against 3NT and the ten wins, East playing the seven. A low diamond comes from dummy, which brings forth the six, jack and queen.

It looks like South has five diamonds (he is known to hold at most two spades, three hearts and, from partner's signal, three clubs) so the contract will make unless partner has an ace and you can find it. Assuming declarer would play for the drop in diamonds if he had six of them, partner is marked with four spades and three hearts. This makes partner more likely to hold a given card in spades than in hearts. Another way to reach the same result is to reason that partner can only have the ♡A if South holds a doubleton ♠A-K, but that several layouts allow partner to have the ♠A.

You cannot read suit-preference into the ♣7 — partner had to signal four — or into the ◇6 since (a) it might be from either ◇9-8-6 or ◇6-x and (b) with ◇10-x, partner can hardly play the ◇10 in case South has ◇K-J-9-x-x.

Bridge logic confirms the attraction of a spade switch. With the ♠A as well as the ♠K, declarer would have had an alternative line of running five rounds of spades. No matter what you discarded, with careful reading declarer could have made his game.

Middle Path

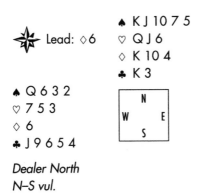

♣ Lead: ◊6

♠ K J 10 7 5
♡ Q J 6
◊ K 10 4
♣ K 3

♠ Q 6 3 2
♡ 7 5 3
◊ 6
♣ J 9 6 5 4

```
        N
   W         E
        S
```

Dealer North
N–S vul.

WEST	NORTH	EAST	SOUTH
	1♠	2◊	2♡
pass	3♡	pass	4♡
all pass			

South, as you will find out in a moment, has a diamond stopper; he might have bid 3NT over 3♡ to offer his partner a choice of contracts if that option had been available. These days many people play that once the partnership has established an eight-card fit in a major, a bid of 3NT is some sort of slam try. It may ask North to cuebid or it is sometimes played as Roman Keycard Blackwood at a level lower than usual. As this deal arose at rubber bridge, the players probably had no such agreement.

You lead your singleton diamond and partner, who has bid diamonds, wins with the ◊A and returns the ◊7. South plays the ◊3 and then the ◊Q, and you ruff that with the ♡5. What do you do now?

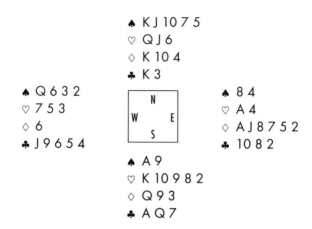

                    ♠ K J 10 7 5
                    ♡ Q J 6
                    ◇ K 10 4
                    ♣ K 3

    ♠ Q 6 3 2   N   ♠ 8 4
    ♡ 7 5 3   W   E   ♡ A 4
    ◇ 6   ◇ A J 8 7 5 2
    ♣ J 9 6 5 4   S   ♣ 10 8 2

                    ♠ A 9
                    ♡ K 10 9 8 2
                    ◇ Q 9 3
                    ♣ A Q 7

You lead a diamond to the ace and East returns the seven, on
which South plays the queen. You ruff with the ♡5.

You don't have to believe South's ◇Q — he could have
another (indeed, depending on the range of your jump overcalls,
you might be able to infer that East does not possess a seven-card
suit). Still, partner's ◇7 seems a little difficult to understand. He
could have afforded a higher diamond if he wanted a spade, his
lowest diamond if he wanted a club. Inspiration! He doesn't want
either of those: his entry lies in the trump suit. If you don't play
a trump now, the declarer will discard a diamond from dummy
on the third club. You will, of course, lead the ♡3 to complete an
echo and so tell partner you want another ruff.

This was a classic suit-preference situation and, in a suit contract, a middle card in a plain suit always indicates neutral preference between the other two plain suits. However, in a notrump
contract, or if the signal comes in the trump suit, a defender
might wish to signal for any of the three remaining suits; in this
case a middle card can ask for the middle suit.

Happy Result

```
          ♠ A 10 3
          ♡ Q J 10
          ◇ K J 7 5
          ♣ J 7 2
                          ♠ J 9
  Lead: ♣3    N          ♡ 8 3 2
            W   E         ◇ Q 10 6 4
                S         ♣ A K 10 4
```

Dealer North
Neither vul.

WEST	NORTH	EAST	SOUTH
	1NT	pass	2♣
pass	2◇	pass	4♠
all pass			

North's 1NT opening was weak, 12-14. South's 2♣ asked for four-card majors and 2◇ denied them. Some people foolishly ask questions to which they don't want to know the answer because they think it is clever to show off their system. South, you know, does not fall into that category; he is a player whose abilities you respect.

Partner leads the ♣3. You win with the ♣K and declarer follows with the ♣5.

How do you think your side might win four tricks? Take careful note of the bidding and picture how the first four tricks might go.

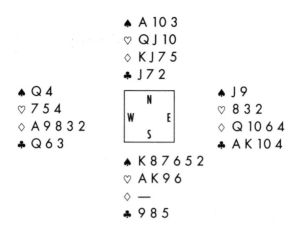

```
                ♠ A 10 3
                ♡ Q J 10
                ◇ K J 7 5
                ♣ J 7 2
  ♠ Q 4            ┌─────┐         ♠ J 9
  ♡ 7 5 4          │  N  │         ♡ 8 3 2
  ◇ A 9 8 3 2      │ W E │         ◇ Q 10 6 4
  ♣ Q 6 3          │  S  │         ♣ A K 10 4
                   └─────┘
                ♠ K 8 7 6 5 2
                ♡ A K 9 6
                ◇ —
                ♣ 9 8 5
```

West leads the three of clubs and you win with the king.

It sounds from the bidding as though South has six spades and four hearts. You don't know whether he is 6-4-1-2 or 6-4-0-3, but it must be safe to return a low club as West wouldn't lead fourth best from four small. West wins with the ♣Q and returns a club, all following.

Judging that South will be void in diamonds and knowing that if West holds the ♡K it cannot run away, you try a thirteenth club and … suddenly you have a trump trick.

On this deal, West has to ruff with the queen to effect the uppercut and ruffing high tends to work best in such positions. However, sometimes you need to save your highest card:

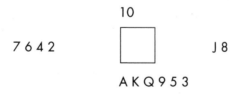

```
            10
          ┌─────┐
  7 6 4 2 │     │ J 8
          └─────┘
          A K Q 9 5 3
```

With a trump suit like this, East wants to ruff with the eight, keeping the jack to cover the ten. Ruffing with the eight also gains if West has 9-x-x, Q-6-x-x or K-7-x. Only if East places South with eight trumps should he ruff with the jack.

Disaster Story

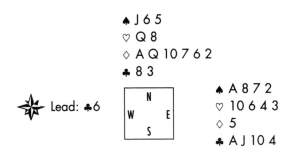

♠ J 6 5
♡ Q 8
◇ A Q 10 7 6 2
♣ 8 3

Lead: ♣6

N
W   E
S

♠ A 8 7 2
♡ 10 6 4 3
◇ 5
♣ A J 10 4

Dealer South
Both vul.

WEST	NORTH	EAST	SOUTH
			1NT
pass	3NT	all pass	

1NT shows 15-17, a fairly standard range for rubber bridge players. Interestingly, however, in the 2003 Bermuda Bowl final, pairs on both the American and Italian teams were using a weak notrump (although only at certain vulnerabilities). A strong notrump tends to protect you from large penalties when partner has a bad hand. This is important at aggregate scoring. However, if you are using a strong notrump, you often find yourself making an opening bid in one of the minors, thereby allowing the opponents an easy entry into the auction. This is a concern both at IMPs and at matchpoints.

West leads the ♣6 to East's ace and South plays the ♣5. In a match between good teams, an identical disaster occurred at both tables. (1) What was it? (2) How might it have been avoided?

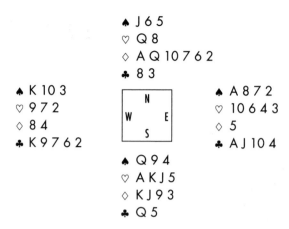

```
                    ♠ J 6 5
                    ♡ Q 8
                    ◇ A Q 10 7 6 2
                    ♣ 8 3
  ♠ K 10 3              N           ♠ A 8 7 2
  ♡ 9 7 2                           ♡ 10 6 4 3
  ◇ 8 4          W         E        ◇ 5
  ♣ K 9 7 6 2            S          ♣ A J 10 4
                    ♠ Q 9 4
                    ♡ A K J 5
                    ◇ K J 9 3
                    ♣ Q 5
```

West leads the ♣6 to East's ace and South plays the ♣5.

The original East returned the ♣J and you can guess what happened next: West, placing declarer with ♣Q-10-5, allowed the queen to hold. South registered +660 instead of -300.

This occurred at both tables and the players agreed that West's play was fair enough. After all, East could have held the ◇K or the ♡A as an entry. They decided that it might have been better for East, with this sort of holding, to return fourth best, the ♣4 on this occasion. The 'rule of eleven' tells him that declarer cannot hold something like ♣Q-9-x and he can see five defensive tricks if his partner wins and returns a club — in practice there are more.

It so happens that if West misreads the club situation he may well take the ♣K and return the ♠10, hoping to find East with ♠Q-9-x or ♠Q-8-7 and the ◇K.

Note that it doesn't help for East to return the ♣10. West will then be even more inclined to hold off, placing the declarer with ♣Q-J-x. Neither, of course, should East lay down the ♠A at the second trick. If West had ♣Q-x-x-x-x and the ♡A or the ♡K, this would hand declarer the contract on a plate.

Quick Move

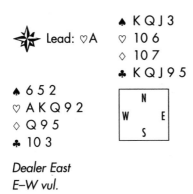

                    ♠ K Q J 3
      Lead: ♡A   ♡ 10 6
                    ◊ 10 7
                    ♣ K Q J 9 5

♠ 6 5 2
♡ A K Q 9 2   N
◊ Q 9 5   W   E
♣ 10 3   S

Dealer East
E–W vul.

WEST	NORTH	EAST	SOUTH
		pass	1NT
pass	2♣	pass	2♠
pass	4♠	all pass	

South's 1NT is announced as weak, 12-14. Even if East were not a passed hand, it would be sheer folly to overcall 2♡ with this shape at this vulnerability. You have no difficulty in passing smoothly (indeed you almost never bid over an opponent's 1NT opening with a 5332 type unless you have sufficient values to double for penalties). When North bids on, you feel hopeful that the opponents will end up in 3NT and that you will cash the first five tricks. Alas, their location of a 4-4 spade fit dashes this hope.

You begin with a top heart, which draws the ♡6, the ♡4 and the ♡5. How do you continue?

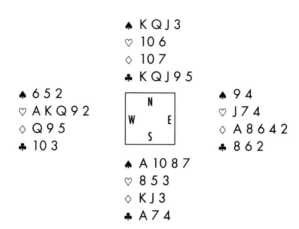

Defending 4♠, you lead a top heart, on which East plays the four and declarer the five.

It would be a mistake to draw another heart and then look around. Scope exists for partner to hold only one ace or king (you can count up to 35 points elsewhere) and two chances present themselves, one slim, one very slim. The very slim chance is that partner holds a singleton club and a black ace (i.e. a singleton ♣A, or a small singleton club and the ♠A). This would give declarer a slightly off-beat 4-2-2-5 shape; you could then switch to a club, get back in with a heart and deliver partner a ruff. The slim chance is that he holds the ◇A and the ♡J. Try for that. Lead a low heart, trusting that East will produce the jack and return a low diamond. Even if declarer places you with the high hearts, he knows that even the ◇A wouldn't give you the 15 points you would need to double 1NT, so he may still misguess.

In retrospect, if partner would have understood your plan, you might have done better to lead the *queen* of hearts initially, allowing partner to encourage if holding the jack.

Either Suit

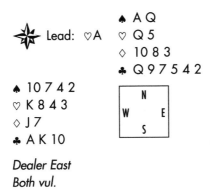

Lead: ♡A

♠ A Q
♡ Q 5
◇ 10 8 3
♣ Q 9 7 5 4 2

♠ 10 7 4 2
♡ K 8 4 3
◇ J 7
♣ A K 10

Dealer East
Both vul.

WEST	NORTH	EAST	SOUTH
		2◇ *	3◇
3♡	4◇	all pass	

East's two diamonds is a 'multi': here a weak two in hearts or spades. It can work well if partner has a good hand, as the stronger, less defined hand, may become declarer. It also frees the opening bids of two hearts and two spades for another purpose, perhaps a different strength single-suited hand or a two-suiter. The real downside is that it gives the opponents two chances to come in — directly over 2◇ and after opener reveals his suit. Also, sometimes you cannot guess partner's suit. The 3◇ overcall is natural and your 3♡ implies that you can play at the three-level in partner's major, whatever it turns out to be.

You lead a top club, on which East plays the ♣6 and declarer the ♣8, and cash a second club, to which all follow. How should you continue?

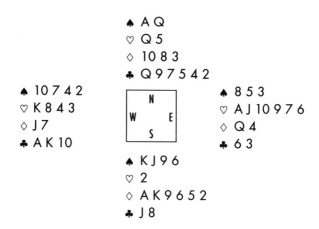

            ♠ A Q
            ♡ Q 5
            ◊ 10 8 3
            ♣ Q 9 7 5 4 2

♠ 10 7 4 2   ┌─────────┐   ♠ 8 5 3
♡ K 8 4 3   │   N   │   ♡ A J 10 9 7 6
◊ J 7   │ W   E │   ◊ Q 4
♣ A K 10   │   S   │   ♣ 6 3
                    └─────────┘
            ♠ K J 9 6
            ♡ 2
            ◊ A K 9 6 5 2
            ♣ J 8

Defending against 4◊, you begin with the ace and king of clubs, to which all follow.

If partner's six-card major is spades, it seems most unlikely that your side will make more than two clubs and a heart (to have overcalled at the three-level, vulnerable, South surely holds a high card in the majors as well as his diamonds, and you do not expect partner to have opened a vulnerable 'multi' on a jack-high suit). If, however, partner has hearts then a good chance exists for a trump promotion. You must, of course, cash the ♡K before leading a third round of clubs. With no loser to discard now, declarer has to overruff East's ◊Q. Your jack will take the setting trick.

Note that the uppercut with the queen would prove equally effective even if declarer unexpectedly held seven trumps (i.e. if partner had four spades on the side).

Upside Down

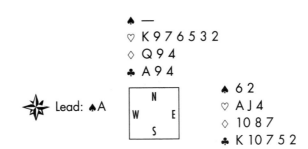

♠ —
♡ K 9 7 6 5 3 2
◇ Q 9 4
♣ A 9 4

Lead: ♠A

♠ 6 2
♡ A J 4
◇ 10 8 7
♣ K 10 7 5 2

Dealer North
E–W vul.

WEST	NORTH	EAST	SOUTH
	3◇	pass	3♡
3♠	4♡	dbl	all pass

North's 3◇ was a De Weerd transfer preempt. Refraining from a feeble pun that must have been heard many times, we will remark simply that it expressed a preempt in the next higher suit. After making such an opening, it is almost invariably wrong to bid one more on the next round. In the East position you decide to teach North a small lesson.

West leads the ♠A (from ♠A-K) and dummy ruffs. A low diamond then goes to the seven, three and jack. Your partner cashes the ◇K, and then leads the ♡10, on which dummy plays low.

Playing the ♡4 looks 'natural', but is it right?

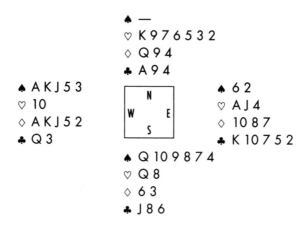

```
                    ♠ —
                    ♡ K 9 7 6 5 3 2
                    ◊ Q 9 4
                    ♣ A 9 4
  ♠ A K J 5 3         ┌─────────┐        ♠ 6 2
  ♡ 10                │    N    │        ♡ A J 4
  ◊ A K J 5 2         │ W     E │        ◊ 10 8 7
  ♣ Q 3               │    S    │        ♣ K 10 7 5 2
                      └─────────┘
                    ♠ Q 10 9 8 7 4
                    ♡ Q 8
                    ◊ 6 3
                    ♣ J 8 6
```

West leads a high spade against 4♡ doubled and dummy ruffs. A low diamond goes to the seven, three and jack. West cashes the king of diamonds (not a very bright play — if both sides attack the same suit, one usually does so in error), and then leads the ten of hearts, on which dummy plays low.

It appears natural, in a sense, to play low, retaining the ♡A-J over dummy's king. All the same, you can be certain that declarer intends to ruff a diamond, so you cannot lose by playing ace of hearts and another. Can you gain? You might, because if you play low on this trick you give South an additional entry.

If you duck, what happens is that declarer wins with the ♡Q and leads a high spade to ruff, forcing West to cover. He ruffs the third diamond and plays another spade, again forcing West to cover. This sequence means that eventually you will have to lead clubs, at the probable cost of a trick in the suit.

You will see that, given the extra entry, South would have made a trick in spades had he held ♠Q-J. On all grounds, it is better on the trump lead to play ace of hearts and another.

Hidden Charm

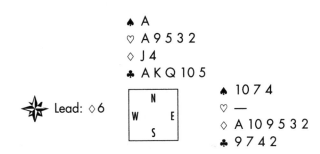

♠ A
♡ A 9 5 3 2
◇ J 4
♣ A K Q 10 5

Lead: ◇6

♠ 10 7 4
♡ —
◇ A 10 9 5 3 2
♣ 9 7 4 2

Dealer South
Neither vul.

WEST	NORTH	EAST	SOUTH
			1♡
pass	4NT	pass	5♣
pass	6♡	all pass	

North-South were playing five-card majors. Afterwards North explained that had his partner shown an ace over 4NT he could have followed, in his system, with a trump-asking bid. If by any chance there were two diamond losers, at least his sequence would not have helped West find the killing lead.

These days most tournament players use Roman Keycard Blackwood, which would help if used here because the ♡K would count as an ace. Over a two keycard response (five hearts), North would probably gamble on the grand slam. He would know that with at least ten trumps in the two hands the queen was likely to fall. He would certainly bid seven if South showed two keycards and the trump queen (with a response of five spades).

On the lead of the ◇6, you play the ◇A and South the ◇Q. What do you return?

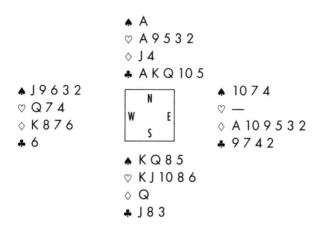

West leads the six of diamonds. When the ◇Q falls under the ace, you first wonder whether this could be a false card from ◇Q-x. Your next inclination may be to ask yourself, 'could my partner hold a void in clubs?' The latter seems improbable because he is not vulnerable and failed to take any sort of action over the 1♡ opening. Also, if hoping for a ruff, he would have led 'top of nothing' rather than a small diamond. Finding him with ◇K-x-x or even a singleton seems a much better chance.

So, you decide to play back a diamond. Which one do you choose? Well, if declarer is going to ruff, returning the two could give you a slight advantage. If your opponent reads this return as fourth best, he will place your partner with six diamonds, hence apparently less room for other cards. Then, if he has a fairly inno-cent nature, he may well misguess the trumps when missing ♡Q-x-x (or even ♡K-x).

Give partner credit for his attacking diamond lead from K-x-x-x. After the confident auction, a more passive spade lead from his longer, weaker suit would not have been so good and his trump holding was wrong for leading the singleton club.

Early Count

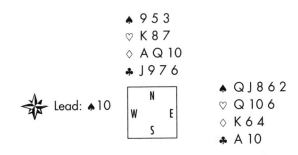

♠ 9 5 3
♡ K 8 7
◇ A Q 10
♣ J 9 7 6

Lead: ♠10

♠ Q J 8 6 2
♡ Q 10 6
◇ K 6 4
♣ A 10

Dealer East
Both vul.

WEST	NORTH	EAST	SOUTH
		1♠	1NT
pass	3NT	all pass	

East may have had no choice as to his opening bid but it raises a point. Have you noticed that people who like a weak notrump shy away from opening 1NT with a five-card major yet strong notrump players think nothing of it? We think we can unravel the mystery. With 12-14, there is a real risk of having a weak suit and a fair chance that the deal revolves around competing for the partscore. This makes it important to find a 5-3 (or 5-4) fit if one exists. You can also keep out of trouble on deals like this! Conversely, holding 15-17 reduces the danger of competition whilst at the same time increasing the chance that partner has sufficient values to inquire about your shape if necessary.

West leads the ♠10 and declarer wins with the ♠K. He lays down the ♣K and you win. He takes the next spade, partner following, and then plays three more clubs.

You have to find two discards. What will they be?

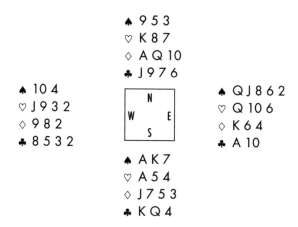

```
                    ♠ 9 5 3
                    ♡ K 8 7
                    ◇ A Q 10
                    ♣ J 9 7 6
  ♠ 10 4            ┌──────────┐      ♠ Q J 8 6 2
  ♡ J 9 3 2         │    N     │      ♡ Q 10 6
  ◇ 9 8 2           │ W      E │      ◇ K 6 4
  ♣ 8 5 3 2         │    S     │      ♣ A 10
                    └──────────┘
                    ♠ A K 7
                    ♡ A 5 4
                    ◇ J 7 5 3
                    ♣ K Q 4
```

West leads the ten of spades; declarer wins and knocks out the ace of clubs. He wins the spade return and plays three more rounds of clubs. You read West for a doubleton spade because with three to the ten he would have led a low card.

Here we see a situation that marks the difference between an average and an expert defender. You can count your opponent for at least top eight tricks — two spades, two hearts, three clubs and one diamond. The danger is that you will be thrown in with the third spade and forced to lead into dummy's diamonds.

This will surely happen if you follow the path of least resistance, discarding one heart and one diamond. The best play is to throw two diamonds on the long clubs. Declarer will continue with the ♡K and the ♡A, on which you will play the ♡6 and the ♡Q or the ♡10 and the ♡Q. At this point declarer may take you for a 5-2-4-2 distribution and exit with a spade, expecting you to be endplayed in diamonds.

A small question: when you discard the diamonds, should you play the ◇6 before the ◇4 or vice versa? Against a moderate declarer the echo, as if you held ◇K-x-x-x, would be right. Against an expert who knows your tricks, it's just a guess.

Guessing Game

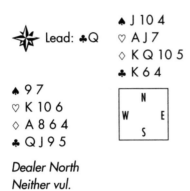

Lead: ♣Q

North
♠ J 10 4
♡ A J 7
◇ K Q 10 5
♣ K 6 4

West
♠ 9 7
♡ K 10 6
◇ A 8 6 4
♣ Q J 9 5

```
    N
 W     E
    S
```

Dealer North
Neither vul.

WEST	NORTH	EAST	SOUTH
	1NT	pass	2♠
all pass			

At rubber bridge, North-South are playing a 12-14 notrump and natural, non-transfer, responses. Though nobody can deny the constructive advantages of transfers (and we recommend that you play them), natural responses pose more problems for the defending side. A transfer bid of 2♡ would give the West hand here additional ways of entering the auction: a cuebid of two spades and a double of the transfer, for example. With this hand, you are too weak to come in anyway.

You lead the ♣Q, covered by the ♣K and the ♣A. East returns the ♣2 and you win with the ♣9, South following with the ♣3 and the ♣8.

What offers you the best chance to defeat the contract?

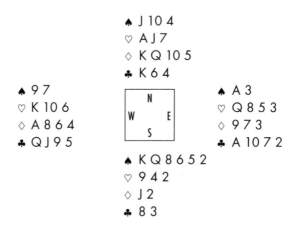

As West, you begin with the queen of clubs, which is covered by the king and ace. Partner returns the two and your nine wins.

It was natural for South to play the ♣K on the first round since players sometimes lead the queen from ace-queen when the bidding makes it likely that dummy holds the king. With ♣10-8-7-3, however, it seems improbable that declarer would have covered, so you tend to place him with a doubleton.

It seems reasonable to hope that partner may have a trump trick, and you can rely on your ◇A. This means that to beat the contract of 2♠ you will presumably need two tricks in hearts and you must take them quickly as the strong diamond suit in dummy will provide discards.

If East has to attack hearts when in with his trump trick, you need to find him with ♡Q-9-x-x. Of course, declarer may intend to play diamonds before trumps and in any case it looks better to broach hearts from your side, beginning with the ♡10. East captures dummy's ♡J with his ♡Q and plays back a low heart.

South might now misguess because West, with ♡10-8-x or ♡10-8, could have played the same way. (Yes, we admit restricted choice buffs will get it right, but many others won't.)

Good Reason

```
                    ♠ K 6 2
                    ♡ A K 5
                    ◇ K J 9 7
                    ♣ A J 5
                              ♠ J 9 4
    ✳ Lead: ♠3    ┌─────┐    ♡ J 9 7 6 2
                  │  N  │    ◇ A Q
                  │W   E│    ♣ 10 7 4
                  │  S  │
                  └─────┘
```

Dealer North
Neither vul.

WEST	NORTH	EAST	SOUTH
	1◇	pass	1NT
pass	3NT	all pass	

South's 1NT shows around 6-9 points and, unless the suit is terrible, it denies a four-card major.

Declarer thinks for a while before playing low from dummy on the spade lead and heads your ♠J with the ♠A. He then runs the ◇8.

This is the first deal of a rubber and you would prefer not to have the opponents score a game so early. How do you aim to prevent them from doing so?

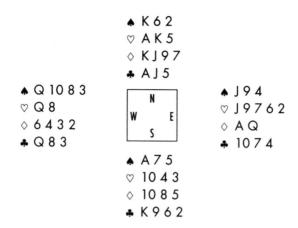

```
                    ♠ K 6 2
                    ♡ A K 5
                    ◇ K J 9 7
                    ♣ A J 5
  ♠ Q 10 8 3        ┌─────────┐      ♠ J 9 4
  ♡ Q 8             │    N    │      ♡ J 9 7 6 2
  ◇ 6 4 3 2         │ W     E │      ◇ A Q
  ♣ Q 8 3           │    S    │      ♣ 10 7 4
                    └─────────┘
                    ♠ A 7 5
                    ♡ 10 4 3
                    ◇ 10 8 5
                    ♣ K 9 6 2
```

West leads a low spade and declarer decides not to hold up,
partly because he would not welcome a heart switch and partly
because the lead of the three (with the two in view) implies a
four-card suit. Having won the spade in hand, he leads the eight
of diamonds and lets it run.

Perhaps you thought to yourself, 'I dare say I'm expected to
win this with the ace, but I can't see any good reason.'

Well, let us tell you the reason. Suppose you win with the ace
and clear the spades. Declarer may come to hand with the ♣K
and lead the ◇10 because from his point of view West might have
begun with ◇Q-x-x-x. The effect of this is that declarer, having
used his club entry to repeat the diamond finesse, will end up
with just two tricks in each suit.

On this occasion it did not matter too much if you had to
think before winning with the ace since it would be natural to
consider a hold up with ◇A-x or ◇A-x-x. All the same, you can
give yourself a bonus point if you noticed the wording 'thinks for
a while' and formed your plan before diamonds were played. The
ability to play in tempo often proves vital.

Messaoe Not Clear

```
              ♠ 10 6
              ♡ Q J 8 4
              ◇ J 9 5
              ♣ 9 7 4 2
                                  ♠ A
        Lead: ◇A      N           ♡ 9 3
                   W     E         ◇ Q 8 7 6 2
                      S            ♣ A J 8 6 3
```

Dealer East
N–S vul.

WEST	NORTH	EAST	SOUTH
		1◇	dbl
1♠	pass	2♣	2♡
2♠	3♡	all pass	

South's sequence, a double followed by the introduction of a new suit, indicates a fairly strong hand but it is not forcing. The requirements have risen over the years. These days one would expect a hand in the region of 18-21 points (or the equivalent, taking account of distribution).

Again in accordance with modern practice West's 1♠ was forcing, in effect ignoring the double. (The traditional approach of starting with a redouble on any good hand exposes you to enemy preemption.)

West leads the ◇A against South's contract of 3♡. As East, what is your defensive plan?

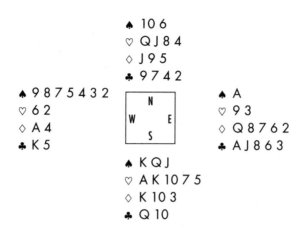

```
              ♠ 10 6
              ♡ Q J 8 4
              ◇ J 9 5
              ♣ 9 7 4 2
♠ 9 8 7 5 4 3 2      ┌─────────┐      ♠ A
♡ 6 2                │    N    │      ♡ 9 3
◇ A 4                │  W   E  │      ◇ Q 8 7 6 2
♣ K 5                │    S    │      ♣ A J 8 6 3
                     └─────────┘
              ♠ K Q J
              ♡ A K 10 7 5
              ◇ K 10 3
              ♣ Q 10
```

West leads the ace of diamonds. The original East, clearly not
wanting a diamond continuation, dropped the ◇2. West then
tried the ♣K and it proved impossible thereafter for the defenders to take more than four tricks.

'If you switch to spades we can take two clubs, a diamond, a
spade, and a ruff,' East pointed out.

'How could I tell that you wanted a spade and not a club?'
West replied. 'You bid clubs and you never supported my spades
even though I bid them twice.'

This was a reasonable answer. Playing East, you should drop
the ◇Q on the first trick instead, obviously an unusual card with
the jack visible in dummy. West will then lead a spade and can
show by means of a suit-preference signal whether he wishes you
to return a club or a diamond. You in turn can play the ♣A and
the ♣8 to partner's ♣K to ensure the spade ruff.

Half Marks

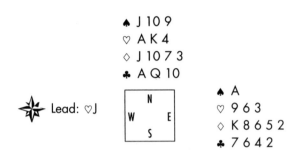

♠ J 10 9
♡ A K 4
◇ J 10 7 3
♣ A Q 10

Lead: ♡J

♠ A
♡ 9 6 3
◇ K 8 6 5 2
♣ 7 6 4 2

Dealer North
Neither vul.

WEST	NORTH	EAST	SOUTH
	1◇	pass	1♠
pass	1NT	pass	2♣
pass	3♠	pass	4♠
all pass			

As you can see, North-South play a weak notrump. Perhaps less obvious is the range for the 1NT rebid, 12-16. 2♣ was 'Crowhurst', asking for range and type; 3♠ showed 15-16 with three spades. An advantage of this method is that you do not have to repeat a five-card suit in a hand too weak to reverse, e.g. with a 1-3-4-5 after 1♣, 1♠, you can rebid 1NT. Among the downsides are (a) responder must often look for game when it is not there, (b) the 2♣ inquiry may reveal vital information about opener's hand if he becomes declarer, and (c) opener must make a 2NT jump rebid with 17 points.

West leads the ♡J (not implying the queen) and dummy wins. The ♠J is led from dummy and you win faultlessly with the ace. What do you next?

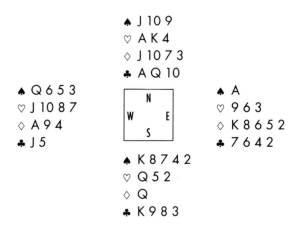

The heart lead against 4♠ goes to dummy's ace and the jack of spades loses to your ace. What should you do now?

Other possibilities do exist, but undoubtedly laying down the ◇K and following with another offers the best chance. As the cards lie, declarer will lose control. When West comes in with the ♠Q, he will play a third round of diamonds, establishing a long trump for your side.

Another possibility is that diamonds are 2-2; in that case a low diamond from East might work better. Well, let's see. If partner has ◇A-x and a trump winner, the contract will fail (unless partner gets it into his head to overtake) regardless of whether you lead high or low; if declarer doesn't have a trump winner, declarer can succeed by ruffing the third round of diamonds high. If South has ◇A-x and cannot discard the loser, you will live or die depending upon whether West has two trump tricks. Again it doesn't matter whether you lead high or low.

The second possibility is that South might hold a lone ◇A and West ♠K-Q-x-x. In this case a low diamond does work better; however, it is more than twice as likely that West has ♠K-x-x-x or ♠Q-x-x-x and South the singleton ◇Q. Sorry, we can't give you more than half marks if you proposed either of those solutions.

Late Discovery

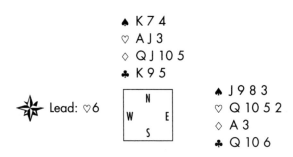

♠ K 7 4
♡ A J 3
◇ Q J 10 5
♣ K 9 5

Lead: ♡6

♠ J 9 8 3
♡ Q 10 5 2
◇ A 3
♣ Q 10 6

Dealer South
Neither vul.

WEST	NORTH	EAST	SOUTH
			1NT[1]
pass	3NT	all pass	

1.   12-14.

West leads the ♡6. Dummy plays low and you win with the ♡10, South playing the ♡4.

The strength of the dummy strikes you as mildly alarming: the opponents have a minimum of 26 points between them, usually sufficient to make a nine-trick game unless the cards lie badly or there is a suit unstopped. The first trick has gone well, but you cannot see any foul breaks lurking for declarer. Can you imagine any possibility of beating South's 3NT contract?

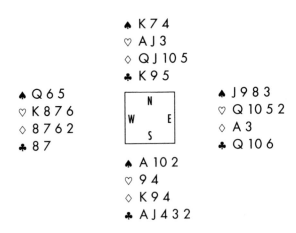

♠ K 7 4
♡ A J 3
◇ Q J 10 5
♣ K 9 5

♠ Q 6 5
♡ K 8 7 6
◇ 8 7 6 2
♣ 8 7

♠ J 9 8 3
♡ Q 10 5 2
◇ A 3
♣ Q 10 6

♠ A 10 2
♡ 9 4
◇ K 9 4
♣ A J 4 3 2

West leads the six of hearts and your ten holds the trick.

If you count the points in dummy and in your own hand, you will conclude that your partner, who presumably holds the ♡K, can hold only 1 or 2 more points: perhaps the ♠Q, perhaps the ♣J. However, the ♣J won't help as this will leave declarer with nine top tricks once he has cleared the diamonds. So let's assume partner holds the ♠Q.

You should begin by misleading declarer about the division of the hearts. Having scored the ♡10, continue with the ♡Q and then the ♡5 (concealing the ♡2). Your opponent will tend to assume now that your partner has led from ♡K-8-7-6-2. Declarer cannot draw any clear inference from the fact that West has apparently not yet played the two. When South discards on the third round, both defenders know the suit's layout, so West would have no need to play the ♡2 (unless he wished to use it to give a suit-preference signal).

Is the light dawning? When you come in with the ◇A, switch to the ♠9 or perhaps play a diamond back. Now South will feel tempted to play the clubs 'for safety'. To keep West out of the lead declarer may play a low club to the nine. You win and, surprise, surprise, find the ♡2 lurking among your diamonds.

Strike Early

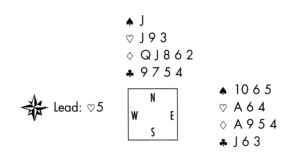

♠ J
♡ J 9 3
◇ Q J 8 6 2
♣ 9 7 5 4

Lead: ♡5

```
      N
  W       E
      S
```

♠ 10 6 5
♡ A 6 4
◇ A 9 5 4
♣ J 6 3

Dealer West
Neither vul.

WEST	NORTH	EAST	SOUTH
pass	pass	pass	2♣
pass	2◇*	pass	2♠
pass	3♣*	pass	4♠
all pass			

North's 2◇ was a waiting bid in the modern style, promising at
least one king or five scattered high card points (2♡ would show
a bust). His rebid of 3♣ indicated a bad hand, and South simply
bid what he thought he could make.

West leads the ♡5 and you win with the ♡A, South following
with the ♡7. What seems to be the best way to dent your opponent's confidence?

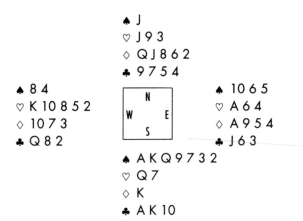

```
              ♠ J
              ♡ J 9 3
              ◇ Q J 8 6 2
              ♣ 9 7 5 4
♠ 8 4                         ♠ 10 6 5
♡ K 10 8 5 2     N           ♡ A 6 4
◇ 10 7 3      W     E        ◇ A 9 5 4
♣ Q 8 2          S           ♣ J 6 3
              ♠ A K Q 9 7 3 2
              ♡ Q 7
              ◇ K
              ♣ A K 10
```

West leads the five of hearts, which you win with the ace. You start by concluding that South has the ♡K or the ♡Q as West would not have underled them both. You can picture South with long strong spades, possibly headed by the ♠A-K-Q, and he surely needs something in clubs as well.

You might think of leading a club up to the weakness in dummy, but is there any need to do that? If you can remove dummy's entry, any possible club loser will not disappear.

Only playing a trump makes sense. Then, if a diamond is led from the table, you can go up with the ace and observe partner's card. If it looks like declarer has unblocked from ◇K-x then you can play a second round, preventing any useful discard (unless South has eight spades, in which case partner will be unable to ruff).

As you predicted, declarer does try a low diamond when he is in dummy with the ♠J. When you see your partner's ◇3 you know that the king is a singleton. (If partner were the one with the singleton he might have led it; besides, declarer would not be playing on the suit before drawing trumps.) In the course of time, you will take four tricks.

Concealed Move

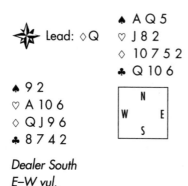

Lead: ◊Q

	♠ A Q 5
	♡ J 8 2
	◊ 10 7 5 2
	♣ Q 10 6

♠ 9 2
♡ A 10 6
◊ Q J 9 6
♣ 8 7 4 2

N
W E
S

Dealer South
E-W vul.

WEST	NORTH	EAST	SOUTH
			1♠
pass	1NT	pass	2♣
pass	3♠	pass	4♠
all pass			

There are other ways of bidding the North hand, but we see nothing much wrong with this sequence. North has suggested a lack of a ruffing value (or he would have raised spades the first time) and implied that South's club rebid has improved his hand.

You lead the ◊Q; ◊4 from partner, ◊8 from the declarer. Several possibilities present themselves now — a diamond to cash more winners or force declarer to ruff — a club perhaps to set up a ruff for partner — or a trump to give nothing away. Which is best?

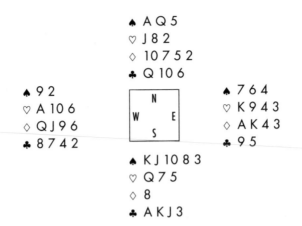

Your lead of the queen of diamonds holds the first trick.

First, how do you read the diamond position? It is difficult to think of any reason why South, holding the ◇A, would hold off the first trick, so you begin by concluding that partner has ◇A-K-x-x or ◇A-K-x.

What about the clubs? If East held a singleton, he would surely overtake the diamond and return a club.

There is a danger attached to leading a second round of diamonds. Your opponent may accept the force and play on reverse dummy lines. As the cards lie, he would be able to ruff three times and still return to dummy to draw the last trump. This would give him ten tricks — three trumps, three ruffs and four clubs.

This makes switching to a trump the expert move; you sit back and wait for three heart tricks. A club switch will also defeat the dummy reversal, although this might spare declarer a guess if East has ♣A-J doubleton. Just hope that your partner will appreciate this ingenious plan.

Second Chance

```
              ♠ K J 8
              ♡ A K 10 3
              ◇ K 7 5
              ♣ J 10 4
                                    ♠ A 7
          Lead: ♠10    ┌─────┐      ♡ J 7 5
                       │  N  │      ◇ 9 4 3
                       │W   E│      ♣ K Q 7 5 3
                       │  S  │
                       └─────┘
```

Dealer North
E–W vul.

WEST	NORTH	EAST	SOUTH
	1NT	pass	3◇
pass	3♡	pass	4◇
pass	4♡	pass	5♣
pass	6◇	all pass	

North-South are playing Precision, 1NT indicating 13-15, and South's response of 3◇ was forcing. 3♡ might initially have been a stopper, which may explain why South delayed his club cue-bid for one round.

Partner leads the ♠10, declarer plays the ♠J from dummy and you win with the ♠A. A club lead would have been more welcome but the bidding has left partner with a straight guess between the black suits; you can hardly blame him for leading from ♠Q-10-9 or ♠10-9 when presumably he holds a collection of low clubs. What seems the best chance now to defeat what may be a borderline slam?

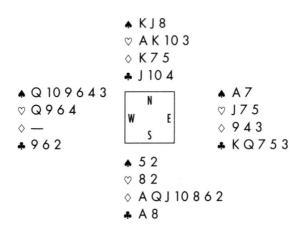

West, unfortunately, leads the ten of spades instead of a club. Dummy plays the jack and your ace wins.

You could switch to the ♣K with a reproachful look, but would this achieve anything? If declarer has a club loser, a club lead now will make no difference and glaring at partner is not good.

What about the major suits? The ♠10 does not seem such a likely lead from ♠10-9-x-x-x-x (the ♠8 is in dummy), so you feel inclined to place partner with ♠Q-10-9. If declarer has the ♡Q, he will have at least eleven tricks on top. Even if he holds only six diamonds, a show-up squeeze will develop when he plays off his winners (West will have to throw spades to keep a heart guard). So, you give partner the ♡Q.

In this type of position, it is nearly always right to attack the dangerous suit, in this case spades. As the cards lie, if you fail to do this, declarer will isolate the menace in hearts by ruffing the third round and West will come under the hammer, holding ♠Q-9 and the ♡Q at the end. Your best return then is a spade. Your side will just survive a torrid endgame. Declarer's club threat is the ♣8 in his own hand and partner can shoulder the burden of covering it. You can take care of the hearts.

Still Alive

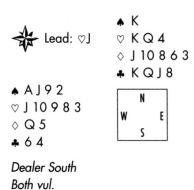

⬥ Lead: ♡J

♠ K
♡ K Q 4
◇ J 10 8 6 3
♣ K Q J 8

♠ A J 9 2
♡ J 10 9 8 3
◇ Q 5
♣ 6 4

N
W   E
S

Dealer South
Both vul.

WEST	NORTH	EAST	SOUTH
			1NT
pass	3NT	all pass	

Playing Precision, South opens 1NT on 13-15, but the hand North puts down is disappointingly strong. You half wonder whether the opponents might have missed a slam — if, for example, South has ◇A-K, the two other aces and a good fit for one of the minors.

You lead the ♡J and dummy's king wins. Then the ◇J runs to your queen. What is your best chance now to show that points are not everything?

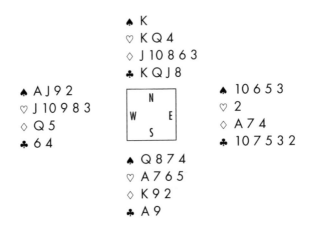

```
                    ♠ K
                    ♡ K Q 4
                    ◊ J 10 8 6 3
                    ♣ K Q J 8
♠ A J 9 2                               ♠ 10 6 5 3
♡ J 10 9 8 3         N                 ♡ 2
◊ Q 5          W         E             ◊ A 7 4
♣ 6 4                    S             ♣ 10 7 5 3 2
                    ♠ Q 8 7 4
                    ♡ A 7 6 5
                    ◊ K 9 2
                    ♣ A 9
```

Declarer wins your lead of the ♡J in dummy and runs the ◊J to your queen.

You could defeat the contract now by laying down the ♠A so long as partner holds ♠Q-x-x-x. Unfortunately, if you make that assumption, you must go further and wonder what declarer is doing, since with the rest of the high cards he would have nine tricks on top (three hearts, two diamonds and four clubs). Thus you should defend on the assumption that partner's one high card is the ◊A.

The original West reached this conclusion but erroneously decided to 'unblock' the spades by leading the ♠9. This might have led to an extra undertrick if South had held ♠Q-10-x; however, as the cards lay the ♠2 would have proved a wiser choice. A switch to the ace fails when South has ♠Q-10-x precisely.

After you have exited with the ♠2 South might play off four rounds of clubs. You have to throw a heart and then a spade, but you still make five tricks by way of two spades, two diamonds and a club.

Best Counter

```
              ♠ 9 5 2
              ♡ A 4
              ◇ 3
              ♣ A Q J 9 8 7 5
                                    ♠ 6 4
    Lead: ♡8      N                 ♡ Q J 10 2
               W     E              ◇ Q 8 4 2
                  S                 ♣ K 10 3
```

Dealer North
E–W vul.

WEST	NORTH	EAST	SOUTH
	1♣	pass	1♠
pass	2♣	pass	2◇
pass	2♠	pass	3NT
pass	4♠	all pass	

Time will tell whether North would have done better to leave his
partner in 3NT. At any rate, South probably did well to offer the
choice as North might have been obliged to bid 2♠ on a doubleton over his forcing 2◇.

West leads the ♡8, which you read as second best from a
weak suit. The ♡10 loses to the ♡K and declarer leads a low club,
which goes to the two, queen, king.

It seems a puzzling situation since you could make a case for
returning any of the four suits. Which is your selection?

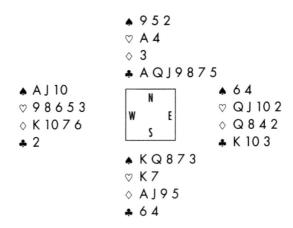

```
              ♠ 9 5 2
              ♡ A 4
              ◇ 3
              ♣ A Q J 9 8 7 5
♠ A J 10          N          ♠ 6 4
♡ 9 8 6 5 3   W     E        ♡ Q J 10 2
◇ K 10 7 6       S           ◇ Q 8 4 2
♣ 2                          ♣ K 10 3
              ♠ K Q 8 7 3
              ♡ K 7
              ◇ A J 9 5
              ♣ 6 4
```

West leads a heart, won by the king. Declarer's first move is a club, which runs to the queen and king, West's ♣2 presumably being a singleton.

At this point various possibilities present themselves: a trump to cut down diamond ruffs; a heart to remove dummy's entry; a diamond to force dummy to ruff (at once or later); a club for partner to ruff.

On a closer look, you can rule out most of the possibilities. A heart will achieve nothing — declarer will just play on trumps and run the clubs later. Nor can a club be right; if West had wanted a ruff, he could have led his singleton. Finally, now that clubs are set up, it can hardly help the defenders to attack trumps.

In a difficult situation like this you should reflect on what declarer is trying to do. Here he wants to establish and run the clubs. The best counter is to play on diamonds to weaken the dummy. After a diamond return, South can do no better than win with the ace and lead a high spade. West wins and leads a diamond, forcing dummy to ruff. Declarer may then try a club; West ruffs and leads another diamond (or a heart will do). One way or another you can always defeat the contract and North will wish he had passed 3NT after all.

fine Reward

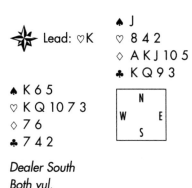

Lead: ♡K

♠ J
♡ 8 4 2
◇ A K J 10 5
♣ K Q 9 3

♠ K 6 5
♡ K Q 10 7 3
◇ 7 6
♣ 7 4 2

```
  N
W   E
  S
```

Dealer South
Both vul.

WEST	NORTH	EAST	SOUTH
			1♠
pass	2◇	pass	2♠
pass	3♣	pass	3NT
all pass			

Since a 2NT rebid by South would have shown extra values, 2♠ did not promise a six-card spade suit. In light of subsequent developments, you feel inclined to place him with either six spades or a 5-3-2-3 shape. If he has very little in the minors, 5-3-3-2 and 5-3-1-4 are also possible.

You lead the ♡K; East plays the ♡5 and South the ♡9. Since you would expect your partner to encourage with the ♡6 from ♡J-6-5 or to unblock with ♡J-5, it looks as though declarer holds ♡A-J-9 and is playing the old *coup de bain*.

As the dummy contains 14 points, it will not be easy to beat this contract. What offers the best chance?

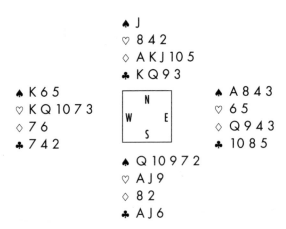

```
              ♠ J
              ♡ 8 4 2
              ◇ A K J 10 5
              ♣ K Q 9 3
♠ K 6 5           N           ♠ A 8 4 3
♡ K Q 10 7 3                  ♡ 6 5
◇ 7 6         W       E       ◇ Q 9 4 3
♣ 7 4 2           S           ♣ 10 8 5
              ♠ Q 10 9 7 2
              ♡ A J 9
              ◇ 8 2
              ♣ A J 6
```

You lead the king of hearts, on which East plays the five and
declarer the nine. You feel pretty sure South has ducked from
♡A-J-9

   You do not intend to continue hearts or shift to diamonds,
that is certain. What about a club switch? There is room (in terms
of points) for partner to hold the ♣A and the ◇Q. No good —
declarer will win the second or third heart, finesse the ◇J and
probably make nine tricks by way of one spade, one heart, four
diamonds and at least three clubs. Play partner for ♣A-J-x, then?
In this case, declarer will surely have the ◇Q and so has eight
tricks on top; furthermore, the discards on the diamonds will
ruin your hand. (True, you might survive if you can convince
declarer to go for his ninth trick in spades rather than diamonds,
perhaps by baring your king.)

   It is never easy to lead from a king into a suit declarer has
rebid but, on balance, a small spade offers you the best hope.
Moreover, it may bring in 300!

Possible Bonus

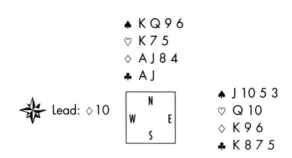

♠ K Q 9 6
♡ K 7 5
◇ A J 8 4
♣ A J

Lead: ◇10

♠ J 10 5 3
♡ Q 10
◇ K 9 6
♣ K 8 7 5

Dealer North
Neither vul.

WEST	NORTH	EAST	SOUTH
	1♣	pass	2♡
pass	3♡	pass	4♡
all pass			

North's 1♣ is Precision, 16 upwards, and South's 2♡ is a semi-positive, usually indicating 3-6 points and a six-card suit. This does not seem to have worked well for them since if South had given a 1◇ negative, North would have rebid 1NT. A transfer bid of 2◇ by South would then have enabled North to be declarer. Generally it proves harder to defend with the strong hand concealed, if for no other reason than that you must start with a lead up to it.

West leads the ◇10 and your king wins. What should you lead to the next trick?

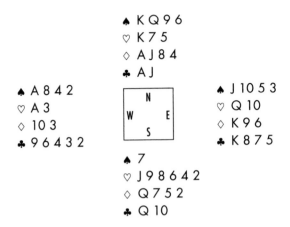

West leads the ten of diamonds and you win with the king. The lead can hardly be a singleton since that would give South 6-5 in the red suits. The danger of continuing diamonds is that declarer will win in hand and lead a spade, setting up discards for his club losers. You may think of returning a club but South is likely to hold the ♣Q. (If he holds the ♡A you cannot defeat the contract and with a jack-high suit he needs the ♣Q for his final bid of 4♡.)

Once you place partner with the ♡A, your best plan is to switch to the ♡10. West will win and lead a club (but not too low a club lest you place him with a singleton diamond, though it makes no difference as the cards lie). This will establish four tricks for your side and a bonus may come: from declarer's point of view you might hold a singleton ♡10, so he may finesse in trumps and go two down.

Against the Odds

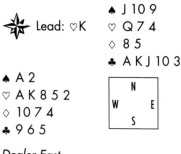

♠ J 10 9
♡ Q 7 4
♢ 8 5
♣ A K J 10 3

♠ A 2
♡ A K 8 5 2
♢ 10 7 4
♣ 9 6 5

Lead: ♡K

Dealer East
Both vul.

WEST	NORTH	EAST	SOUTH
		pass	1♠
pass	2♣	pass	2♢
pass	3♠	pass	4♠
all pass			

Although you might have overcalled in hearts, you quite rightly passed, vulnerable and facing a passed partner. You have a balanced hand and the aces and king offer good defensive prospects. North's jump preference to 3♠ was invitational.

You lead the ♡K (or the ♡A), on which partner plays the ♡3 and declarer the ♡9. With the ♡Q on display in dummy, you read partner's ♡3 as a count signal, showing an odd number of hearts. This is not a promising start, or so it seems. How do you continue?

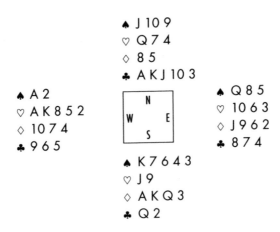

```
                    ♠ J 10 9
                    ♡ Q 7 4
                    ◇ 8 5
                    ♣ A K J 10 3
♠ A 2                                    ♠ Q 8 5
♡ A K 8 5 2        ┌─────────┐          ♡ 10 6 3
◇ 10 7 4           │ W   N   E │         ◇ J 9 6 2
♣ 9 6 5            │     S     │         ♣ 8 7 4
                   └─────────┘
                    ♠ K 7 6 4 3
                    ♡ J 9
                    ◇ A K Q 3
                    ♣ Q 2
```

You lead a high heart and when East plays the three you know
that dummy's queen will be a trick. Since declarer might discard
his remaining heart on dummy's clubs, you should work out that
there is nothing better than to lead a second heart and, when East
plays low again, a third. (If he followed up with his higher heart,
you would shift to a diamond, placing him with the ◇A or
◇K-Q).

After the ♡Q wins, the ♠9 runs to your ace. Hoping partner
has ♠Q-8 left, you try a fourth heart. Dummy ruffs and East discards. The contract goes one down — against all the odds!

Although here East's threat to ruff with the ♠8 was vital, a
ruff and discard can have a deadly effect on more solid opposing
trumps (so long as the defenders have taken their side winners).
Here declarer (or dummy) has already been forced to ruff once:

```
              J 10 7
          ┌─────────┐
    A     │         │     Q 6 4 3
          └─────────┘
              K 9 8 5
```

When West takes the jack with the ace and continues the force,
declarer is lost. No matter which hand he ruffs in, he will be
unable to pick up East's queen.

Nothing Lost

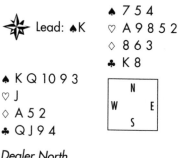

✦ Lead: ♠K

♠ 7 5 4
♡ A 9 8 5 2
◇ 8 6 3
♣ K 8

♠ K Q 10 9 3
♡ J
◇ A 5 2
♣ Q J 9 4

N
W   E
S

Dealer North
Both vul.

WEST	NORTH	EAST	SOUTH
	pass	pass	1NT
pass	2◇ *	pass	3♡
pass	4♡	all pass	

You would certainly have bid over 1NT if your methods allowed you to show spades and clubs. You might have tried a natural 2♠ even without that option. Perhaps your plan was to compete on the next round if the opponents were in 2♡. When the opponents press on to game, however, you are probably relieved to have stayed out of the auction. South's 3♡ bid was a super-accept of the transfer, showing four hearts and a maximum notrump opening (17 HCP).

You lead the ♠K, on which East plays the ♠2 and South the ♠6. With four spades declarer would surely have won the first trick so you place him with ♠A-J-6. You try the ♣Q but declarer wins with the ace, draws trumps in three rounds (you discard spades), leads the ♣10 to dummy's king and returns the ◇3. East plays the jack and South the king. How do you defend?

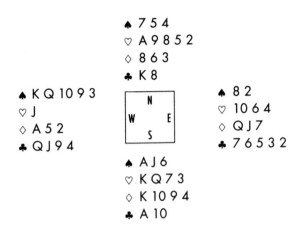

```
              ♠ 7 5 4
              ♡ A 9 8 5 2
              ◇ 8 6 3
              ♣ K 8
♠ K Q 10 9 3   ┌───────────┐   ♠ 8 2
♡ J            │     N     │   ♡ 10 6 4
◇ A 5 2        │  W     E  │   ◇ Q J 7
♣ Q J 9 4      │     S     │   ♣ 7 6 5 3 2
              └───────────┘
              ♠ A J 6
              ♡ K Q 7 3
              ◇ K 10 9 4
              ♣ A 10
```

After your lead of the king of spades holds the first trick, you switch to a club. Declarer wins in hand with the ace of clubs, draws trumps, crosses to the king of clubs, and returns the ◇3 to the jack and king.

It may seem natural to win with the ace, but doing so will eventually enable your opponent to discard dummy's losing spade on the long diamond. Nothing can be lost if you allow the ◇K to hold. Partner will win the second diamond and his spade return will ensure four defensive tricks.

While you might have achieved the same effect by leading a low diamond at the second trick, there is a danger attached to this. If partner has ◇J-10-x and a trump trick, you will be sparing declarer a guess of whether to lead towards his king and queen (hoping for the ace onside) or to take a deep finesse of the nine (playing East for the jack and ten).

Finally, two small points: (1) if East had played the queen of diamonds instead of the jack, you might have placed him with ◇Q-J-10; and (2) East might have played his lowest club on the second (or even the first) round of clubs as a suit-preference signal denoting diamond values, which would also have been helpful to you.

Points of View

```
              ♠ J 8
              ♡ 4
              ◇ J 10 7 5 3
              ♣ K 9 8 5 2
                    ┌─────────┐      ♠ 7 4
  Lead: ♡10         │    N    │      ♡ A Q J 7 6 2
                    │ W     E │      ◇ A Q
                    │    S    │      ♣ 10 7 6
                    └─────────┘
```

Dealer East
E–W vul.

WEST	NORTH	EAST	SOUTH
		1♡	dbl
pass	2◇	pass	2♠
pass	3♠	pass	4♠
all pass			

With a sound opening bid and a decent six-card suit, East's pass over 2◇ appears a trifle cautious, although the adverse vulnerability perhaps played a part. Defending at the two-level when the opponents have a fit rarely works well. Perhaps East had picked up the vibes of a good hand on his left and sensed that the bidding was not about to die.

We have some sympathy with North's 3♠. He thought that 3♣, suggesting a weak minor two-suiter, might be passed and that his singleton heart and support for spades justified a raise.

West led the ♡10 and East won with the ace. What would you have led to the next trick?

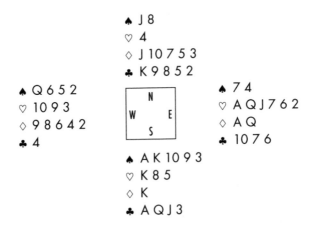

```
              ♠ J 8
              ♡ 4
              ◇ J 10 7 5 3
              ♣ K 9 8 5 2
♠ Q 6 5 2          N          ♠ 7 4
♡ 10 9 3       W       E      ♡ A Q J 7 6 2
◇ 9 8 6 4 2        S          ◇ A Q
♣ 4                           ♣ 10 7 6
              ♠ A K 10 9 3
              ♡ K 8 5
              ◇ K
              ♣ A Q J 3
```

The original East returned a trump and declarer had no difficulty in landing ten tricks — four trumps, five clubs and a heart.

Everyone had something to say:

South: 'I don't know why you didn't show your clubs. Five clubs is laydown.'

North: 'You could have bid your clubs over my spade raise. Your spade support wasn't that good. Since neither my two diamonds nor your two spades was forcing, I would have known that four clubs was a suit, not a cuebid.'

East: 'Why didn't you lead your singleton club? Your queen of spades is likely to be a stopper, so all you need is to find me with two aces.'

West: 'I thought a forcing game might work best. Anyway, what was the point of your spade return? This could hardly produce more than three tricks. The only real hope was to find me with a trump trick and a singleton club. You must return a club and then I score a ruff as the setting trick.'

Did you find the club switch? West was right in saying that at that point in the hand it was the only hope. You can discuss the opening lead with him later!

Start Looking

Lead: ♠3

♠ 9 8
♡ A 7 5 3
♢ K Q 8 5
♣ 9 5 2

♠ A 10 5 3 2
♡ Q J
♢ 6 4
♣ K 7 4 3

```
      N
  W       E
      S
```

Dealer North
N–S vul.

WEST	NORTH	EAST	SOUTH
	pass	pass	1NT[1]
pass	2♣	pass	2♢
pass	3NT	all pass	

1. 15-17.

Over 2♢, North may have stretched to bid the vulnerable game because he knows that the less the auction reveals about declarer's hand the greater the chance of the contract's success.

Sitting West, you lead the ♠3, which runs to the eight, jack and king. Declarer leads the ♢7 to dummy's king, on which East plays the ♢2. Declarer returns a low club, covered with the ♣8 from East and the queen from South.

Do you hold off or do you win with the king? If you win, what will you play next?

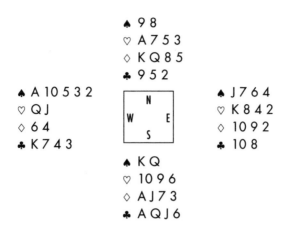

```
              ♠ 9 8
              ♡ A 7 5 3
              ◇ K Q 8 5
              ♣ 9 5 2
♠ A 10 5 3 2        ┌─────┐        ♠ J 7 6 4
♡ Q J              │  N  │        ♡ K 8 4 2
◇ 6 4              │W   E│        ◇ 10 9 2
♣ K 7 4 3          │  S  │        ♣ 10 8
                   └─────┘
              ♠ K Q
              ♡ 10 9 6
              ◇ A J 7 3
              ♣ A Q J 6
```

Defending 3NT, you lead the three of spades, which is covered by the eight, jack and king. The declarer crosses to the king of diamonds and leads a low club to the queen.

As West, you can draw a number of conclusions. Firstly, East does not hold the ◇A — he would have won the first round of the suit in order to play a spade. Secondly, it looks like declarer has four winners in diamonds (because partner's ◇2 indicates an odd number). Thirdly, it is dangerous to refuse to win the club because if South has the ♡K he may be able to run nine tricks without needing to risk losing the lead again.

Having decided to win with the ♣K, you recount the opposing tricks: a spade and a heart you know about, probably four diamonds, and partner's ♣8 (from a doubleton it would seem) looks sinister. There is not much doubt — you must lay down the ♠A. If partner, from an original holding of ♠Q-J-x, fails to unblock, you should look for a new partner.

Last Hurdle

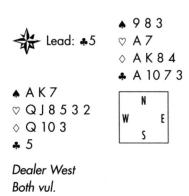

Lead: ♣5

♠ 9 8 3
♡ A 7
◇ A K 8 4
♣ A 10 7 3

♠ A K 7
♡ Q J 8 5 3 2
◇ Q 10 3
♣ 5

N
W   E
S

Dealer West
Both vul.

WEST	NORTH	EAST	SOUTH
1♡	dbl	2♡	3♠
pass	4♠	all pass	

East's raise suggests either four-card heart support in a near bust
— in which event you are not going to defeat the contract — or
three-card support and a few values.

Although singleton leads often backfire, with two trump
entries and an idea of how you might put partner in, the choice
here appears justified: you lead the ♣5. Declarer takes East's
queen with the king and advances the ♠4.

Do you go up with the king? If you do, how will you defend
later on in the play? We would like a full answer.

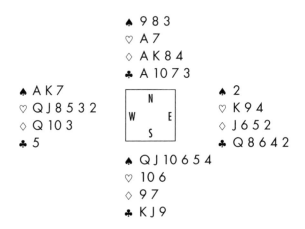

♠ 9 8 3
♡ A 7
◇ A K 8 4
♣ A 10 7 3

♠ A K 7
♡ Q J 8 5 3 2
◇ Q 10 3
♣ 5

N
W E
S

♠ 2
♡ K 9 4
◇ J 6 5 2
♣ Q 8 6 4 2

♠ Q J 10 6 5 4
♡ 10 6
◇ 9 7
♣ K J 9

You lead your singleton club and must decide what to do when declarer attacks trumps.

For sure, it makes sense to follow through with your initial plan and go up with the ♠K. It seems unlikely that East has a singleton queen. Even if he does, you will need another trick — the ♡K no doubt — in which case you should get a ruff to compensate. To make your intentions clear to your partner you then switch to your lowest heart, the two.

The original player who held the West hand got this far. Can you imagine what happened next? Sensing what was coming, declarer called for dummy's ace and played three rounds of diamonds, discarding a heart on the third. West found that he had fallen at the last hurdle because he had to win this trick with his queen. He had no way to reach East's hand.

You should drop the queen on the first or second round of diamonds and unblock the ten as well. This way, East will win the third diamond if declarer goes for the loser-on-loser play.

Interesting Thought

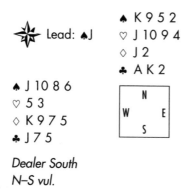

✦ Lead: ♠J

♠ K 9 5 2
♡ J 10 9 4
◇ J 2
♣ A K 2

♠ J 10 8 6
♡ 5 3
◇ K 9 7 5
♣ J 7 5

Dealer South
N–S vul.

WEST	NORTH	EAST	SOUTH
			1NT[1]
pass	2♣	pass	2♡
pass	4♡	all pass	

1. 15-17.

On this sequence, either opponent may have four spades as well as four hearts and you could make a case for a trump lead. Apart from the danger of giving away a trick if you attack spades, you expect your left-hand opponent to produce a ruffing value or he would simply have raised to 3NT.

In practice, you decide to put these thoughts aside and lead the ♠J, which holds. How should you continue?

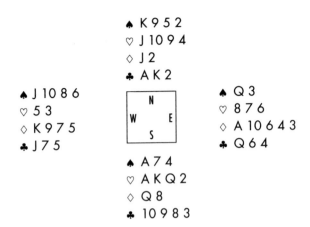

Your opening lead of the jack of spades holds. How should you continue?

The original West placed East with ♠A-Q-x and decided to continue the suit. This time declarer took the ace, collecting East's queen on the way, drew trumps and took the marked spade finesse. He then threw a diamond on the fourth round of spades and made the contract.

If you think carefully, it can hardly help to find East with ♠A-Q. Even assuming that he has three clubs to the queen, your side will only score three tricks. If South holds ◇A-Q-x, the third diamond will take care of dummy's low club. Only in the unlikely event that South is 2-4-2-5, with all his values in the red suits, will continuing spades bear fruit.

By far your best chance is to play East for the ◇A and switch to the suit. You make the first three tricks and a club provides the setting trick. Interestingly, if the contract were 3NT and the play started off the same way (i.e. if declarer rejected the genuine chance of taking the double club finesse), you would still need to find the diamond switch.

Guess What

♠ K 9 8
♡ K J 9 4
◇ 7 4
♣ K J 9 7

Lead: ♠4

♠ A 10 7
♡ 10 3
◇ K J 9 6
♣ 10 5 4 3

Dealer West
N–S vul.

WEST	NORTH	EAST	SOUTH
pass	pass	pass	1NT
pass	2♣	pass	2◇
pass	3NT	all pass	

Partner leads the ♠4 and you instinctively read this as coming from a five-card suit. A lead from a four-card spade suit would be unattractive when dummy might also have four. In any case, the ♠2 and the ♠3 are missing.

When dummy plays low you could grab your ace and switch to diamonds, or maybe something can be done with the spades. What is your plan?

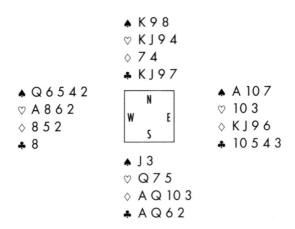

```
                    ♠ K 9 8
                    ♡ K J 9 4
                    ◊ 7 4
                    ♣ K J 9 7
♠ Q 6 5 4 2         ┌──────────┐      ♠ A 10 7
♡ A 8 6 2           │    N     │      ♡ 10 3
◊ 8 5 2             │ W     E  │      ◊ K J 9 6
♣ 8                 │    S     │      ♣ 10 5 4 3
                    └──────────┘
                    ♠ J 3
                    ♡ Q 7 5
                    ◊ A Q 10 3
                    ♣ A Q 6 2
```

After West leads the four of spades and a low card is played from dummy, the ball lands in your court.

It is hard to justify going up with the ace in order to switch to a diamond. For the strategy to work, you would really need to find West with ◊A-10-x-x. It is much more likely that South has the diamond length. You believe he has only two spades and three hearts, which means that unless West has a void in clubs South will hold at least four diamonds.

What happens if you finesse the ♠10? You expect this to lose and, when partner gets in, he will lead another low spade. Unluckily for you, declarer will very often guess correctly since he knows you would have played the queen from ♠Q-10-x. Even if he holds the ♠Q and you play the ♠10 smoothly, the natural thing (on restricted choice grounds, if nothing else) will be to play you for ♠A-10-x rather than ♠J-10-x.

You need to test your opponent more ingeniously. Go up with the ♠A and return the ♠7. From declarer's point of view, you could easily have ♠A-7-x and the ♡A entry. In that case, it would be right for him to save dummy's king for the third round. On the actual layout, however, he goes down if he does so.

Amber Gambler

```
              ♠ J 10
              ♡ A J 10 9 6
              ◇ A K 3
              ♣ Q 9 7
                  ┌─────────┐        ♠ A 5 3
    Lead: ♣5      │    N    │        ♡ K 7 3 2
                  │ W     E │        ◇ 10 8 2
                  │    S    │        ♣ A J 2
                  └─────────┘
```

Dealer South
Both vul.

WEST	NORTH	EAST	SOUTH
			3♠
pass	4♠	all pass	

South comes from the old school and unquestionably his vulnerable preempt means a seven-card suit. Dummy looks quite strong and you may well need to be on your toes to defeat this contract.

West leads the ♣5 and you finesse the ♣J to win the trick. You cash the ♣A and partner follows with the ♣4. How should you defend from here?

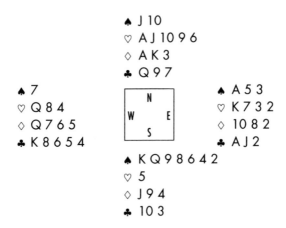

♠ J 10
♥ A J 10 9 6
♦ A K 3
♣ Q 9 7

♠ 7
♥ Q 8 4
♦ Q 7 6 5
♣ K 8 6 5 4

♠ A 5 3
♥ K 7 3 2
♦ 10 8 2
♣ A J 2

♠ K Q 9 8 6 4 2
♥ 5
♦ J 9 4
♣ 10 3

You start with two club tricks against South's 4♠ contract. Partner's high-low tells you that declarer can ruff the third club, which means you must look elsewhere for the setting trick.

On a good day you might defeat the contract even if South has the ◊Q. You would have to hope that card is singleton and switch to a heart whilst the diamonds are blocked. More likely West has the ◊Q, in which case a heart singleton in South's hand presents the main danger. If you defend passively — say by playing a third club — declarer has time to ruff three hearts in hand and eventually enjoy the long card in the suit.

If you are prepared to gamble on finding West with the ◊9, you could switch to the suit. Luckily, a safer strategy exists. Lead a small spade to remove dummy's trump entry whilst keeping yours. Then, if declarer takes two rounds of hearts and plays a trump back, you take the ♠A and revert to clubs. Do you see why? If the ♣Q stayed in dummy it could function as one of the threats for a squeeze against partner in the minors.

Early Exit

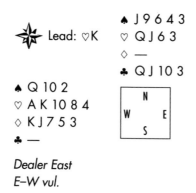

Lead: ♡K

♠ J 9 6 4 3
♡ Q J 6 3
◇ —
♣ Q J 10 3

♠ Q 10 2
♡ A K 10 8 4
◇ K J 7 5 3
♣ —

N
W E
S

Dealer East
E–W vul.

WEST	NORTH	EAST	SOUTH
		3♣	3♠
pass	4♠	all pass	

Some people would double 4♠ on the basis that East's opening preempt has already tipped declarer off about the distribution and that the contract is unlikely to make any overtricks. We regard a double that rates to turn a penalty of 50 into 100 as unsound. If an opponent happens to have a singleton heart, or if strong spades come down in dummy, your hand might make only two tricks and you could lose far more than the 50 points you stood to gain. Besides, how would you feel if, following a double, declarer tackled ♠J-x-x-x-x-x facing ♠A-K-9-x in dummy by taking the double finesse?

You lead a top heart and partner plays the ♡7 — no doubt top of a doubleton. Can you find a good continuation?

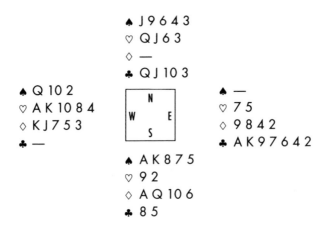

```
                    ♠ J 9 6 4 3
                    ♡ Q J 6 3
                    ◊ —
                    ♣ Q J 10 3
  ♠ Q 10 2                          ♠ —
  ♡ A K 10 8 4       N             ♡ 7 5
  ◊ K J 7 5 3    W       E         ◊ 9 8 4 2
  ♣ —                S              ♣ A K 9 7 6 4 2
                    ♠ A K 8 7 5
                    ♡ 9 2
                    ◊ A Q 10 6
                    ♣ 8 5
```

A top heart wins the first trick, leaving you in the hot seat.

In a teams match the first West blithely continued with two more rounds of hearts. Surprise, surprise, East was unable to ruff the third round and declarer's club losers went away. The other West appreciated that East must have a void in trumps and shifted to the ◊J. He planned to allow dummy to win the second round of hearts, sacrificing his other heart winner in the hope that East would score two clubs. This was a better idea and forced declarer to earn his keep.

South threw a club from dummy on the diamond switch and won with the queen. Next he laid down a top trump, exposing the position, led a heart to the ♡10 and the ♡J, and then ruffed a heart. Next he ruffed a diamond and exited to West by throwing a club on the ♡Q. West escaped this time with a diamond but he was obliged to give a ruff and discard when he got back in with his master trump.

At the second trick, only one precise card defeats the contract: the ♡10. Although declarer gets a heart trick, he is one entry and one trump short to complete the strip and endplay. Whatever he does now, he will lose two clubs and a spade in addition to the heart at Trick 1.

Only the Best

Lead: ♠4

```
            ♠ Q 7 3
            ♡ A 8
            ◇ Q
            ♣ K Q 8 7 6 5 3
♠ 4
♡ J 10 5           ┌─────────┐
◇ 10 8 7 6 5 3 2   │    N    │
♣ A 10             │ W     E │
                   │    S    │
                   └─────────┘
```

Dealer South
Both vul.

WEST	NORTH	EAST	SOUTH
			1♡
pass	2♣	2♠	3♡
pass	4♡	all pass	

Even though you play weak jump overcalls, you would need a significantly better suit than this to bid 3◇, especially when vulnerable. After all, you would hardly open this hand at the three-level. Although it is true that South's opening bid increases the chance that the deal belongs to the opponents, it also gives North vital information and so reduces the effectiveness of any preemptive action on your part.

You lead the ♠4 and are happy to see partner win this with the ♠10. He then proceeds to cash the ♠K and the ♠A. Surely a fourth defensive trick will not elude you.

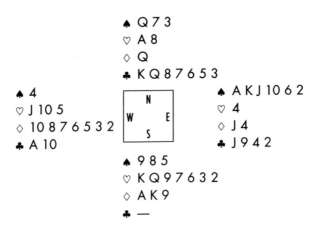

You lead your singleton and partner wins the first three spade tricks, giving you two discards to make.

Plenty of defenders would discard a couple of discouraging diamonds and wait for their partner to lead a club at the next trick. They could scarcely imagine that declarer's club loser, if he has one, can run away. Can you?

If you leave partner on lead, he may think you want him to do something that you cannot do yourself, namely play a fourth round of spades. If you did have ♡Q-9-x, this would be just what the doctor ordered. However, while ruffing the third spade is a good idea, it is not good enough. Only the best will do.

South is known to hold three spades, presumably the top diamonds and, to have rebid 3♡ on minimal values, seven hearts. This leaves him with only one other card — but there's no need to assume it's a club. Happily, you can cater for a possible club void by ditching both your clubs. A club switch then ensures you a trump trick.

Spare Card

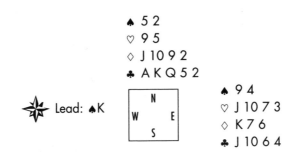

```
              ♠ 5 2
              ♡ 9 5
              ◇ J 10 9 2
              ♣ A K Q 5 2
                                    ♠ 9 4
         Lead: ♠K      N            ♡ J 10 7 3
                    W     E         ◇ K 7 6
                       S            ♣ J 10 6 4
```

Dealer West
Both vul.

WEST	NORTH	EAST	SOUTH
2♠	pass	pass	2NT
pass	3NT	all pass	

Partner's weak two appears to pose few problems for the opposition and they cruise into the notrump game.

West leads the ♠K and, since declarer ducks twice, partner continues with the ♠J and the ♠10, a small heart being thrown from dummy.

You are unsure whether your opponent has held up his ace for an extra round because he does not trust West to turn up with a six-card suit or because he wants to force you into an early discard. If the latter, he has succeeded. What card can you spare?

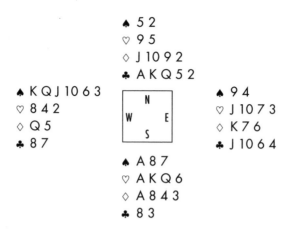

```
              ♠ 5 2
              ♡ 9 5
              ◇ J 10 9 2
              ♣ A K Q 5 2
♠ K Q J 10 6 3        ┌─────────┐        ♠ 9 4
♡ 8 4 2               │    N    │        ♡ J 10 7 3
◇ Q 5                 │ W     E │        ◇ K 7 6
♣ 8 7                 │    S    │        ♣ J 10 6 4
                      └─────────┘
              ♠ A 8 7
              ♡ A K Q 6
              ◇ A 8 4 3
              ♣ 8 3
```

West leads the ♠K and since declarer ducks twice, partner continues with the ♠J and the ♠10, a small heart being thrown from dummy.

One glance at dummy tells you to retain all of your clubs; a heart discard appears highly dangerous as well. It seems quite plausible that declarer has ♡A-K-Q-x as partner can have few high cards outside of spades. It looks like you can spare a low diamond, but watch what happens. . .

After winning the spade perforce, declarer tries three rounds of clubs to test the suit. When West shows out declarer will play the ◇J from dummy and you will probably duck. Alas, it makes no difference as your opponent has a good count on your hand: since you started with six black cards and at least four hearts, there is no room for you to have four diamonds to the king-queen. He will therefore rise with the ace and return the suit, hoping that you have the king rather than the queen. His wish comes true and the contract makes.

West's ♠J continuation — the middle card of his remaining ♠Q-J-10 — looks like a signal for diamonds. Besides, you are hardly ever going to beat the contract if the ◇A-Q lies over your king. Throw the king of diamonds.

Marked Cards

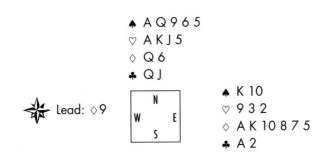

♠ A Q 9 6 5
♡ A K J 5
◇ Q 6
♣ Q J

Lead: ◇9

N
W E
S

♠ K 10
♡ 9 3 2
◇ A K 10 8 7 5
♣ A 2

Dealer East
E–W vul.

WEST	NORTH	EAST	SOUTH
		1◇	pass
pass	dbl	2◇	pass
pass	dbl	pass	2♠
all pass			

North has bid well. His second double showed quite a good hand and he was right to respect South's weak response.

West leads the ◇9 and you win the first two tricks with the ◇K and the ◇A. All follow low, leaving South's ◇J as the master.

It looks like the opponents have a nine-card trump fit (South would no doubt have called 2♡ on ♡Q-x-x or ♡Q-10-x rather than 2♠ on ♠J-x-x or ♠8-x-x). It is not going to be easy to defeat them at the two-level. Do you have any ideas?

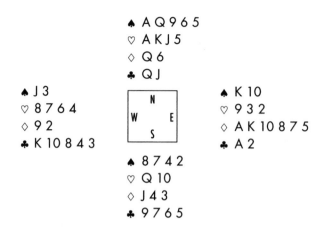

Defending two spades, you win the first two tricks in diamonds.

The original East correctly placed West with the ♣K and switched to ace followed by another club. On the third round, East innocently overruffed the ♠9 with the ♠10 and exited with a heart. Declarer won this in hand, played a spade to the ace and claimed the rest of the tricks.

'Bravo,' exclaimed North, amidst a round of applause from the kibitzers. 'Yes it was well done,' said West, 'but we could have done better.'

'You had better explain that,' replied East, 'I don't follow.'

'Once I turned up with the ♣K, you were marked with the king of trumps, but I could have had ♠ J-10-x, couldn't I?'

Suddenly it dawned on East what he had missed. He should have overruffed the ♠9 with the ♠K rather than the ♠10. From declarer's point of view, East's shape could easily have been 1-4-6-2. East would not have bothered to mention four miserable hearts after North's takeout double.

Dual Danger

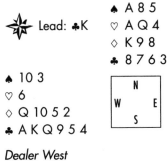

Lead: ♣K

♠ A 8 5
♡ A Q 4
◇ K 9 8
♣ 8 7 6 3

♠ 10 3
♡ 6
◇ Q 10 5 2
♣ A K Q 9 5 4

```
      N
  W       E
      S
```

Dealer West
Both vul.

WEST	NORTH	EAST	SOUTH
1♣	pass	1♠	2♡
pass	4♡	all pass	

In tournament play, North could cuebid 2♠ on the way to 4♡ to say that he is bidding on high cards rather than a stack of hearts. At the rubber bridge table, one dispenses with such niceties. The way that the auction has progressed, you begin to wonder whether you might have fared better by opening a heavy 3♣ — probably not.

You lead a top club and are pleased to see partner signal with the ♣2 — clearly a singleton. This gives you two tricks and you need to find two more. How should you proceed?

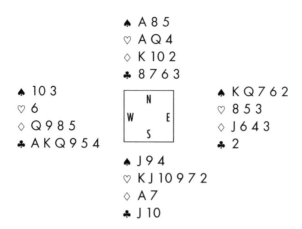

                    ♠ A 8 5
                    ♡ A Q 4
                    ◇ K 10 2
                    ♣ 8 7 6 3

    ♠ 10 3   ♠ K Q 7 6 2
    ♡ 6   ┌─────────┐   ♡ 8 5 3
    ◇ Q 9 8 5   │   N   │   ◇ J 6 4 3
    ♣ A K Q 9 5 4   │ W   E │   ♣ 2
                    │   S   │
                    └─────────┘
                    ♠ J 9 4
                    ♡ K J 10 9 7 2
                    ◇ A 7
                    ♣ J 10

You cash one top club and know a second will score.

An unthinking player will cash the second club and shift to a spade. Although East will win the spade when declarer ducks in dummy, he will be unable to return the suit and can do no better than switch to diamonds. Declarer can then win with the ace, cash two rounds of trumps, unblock the ♠A and finish the trumps. West has to keep a club and East a spade, leaving nobody able to protect diamonds.

The double squeeze is reasonably easy to foresee. South rates to have a six-card suit for his overcall and he must have other values, quite probably the ◇A. Alas, it does you no good to shift to the ◇9 after cashing two clubs. Declarer wins in hand and again runs his trumps. This squeezes East down to a singleton diamond, so now declarer crosses to the ◇K and leads a spade up to the jack to endplay East.

To remove both options you must lead a spade immediately. East will win and return a low diamond. Now you can counter anything declarer does. If he gives up a club, you continue diamonds. If not, partner can keep a diamond as an exit card. Only if East has ◇A-J-x-x and an inspired declarer brings off a strip squeeze will this strategy cost.

Easy Life

★ Lead: ♡5

```
          ♠ 10 7 5 3
          ♡ —
          ◊ 9 6 5 4
          ♣ A K Q 9 3
♠ A K 8 4
♡ J 6 5        ┌─────────┐
◊ J 8 3        │    N    │
♣ 8 5 4        │ W     E │
               │    S    │
               └─────────┘
```

Dealer East
Neither vul.

WEST	NORTH	EAST	SOUTH
		2♡	2NT
pass	3♡	pass	3NT
all	pass		

A 2NT overcall over a weak two can cover quite a wide range. Normally you would expect similar values to a strong notrump opener, but sometimes a player who bids it will be stuck and have 18 or even as many as 19 points. With his cuebid, North was no doubt hoping that South would introduce a suit, ideally spades; this did not happen.

You lead the ♡5 and partner wins with the ♡Q. He returns the ♡7 and you capture declarer's ♡9 with the ♡J, dummy discarding a second spade. What is the best way for you to continue?

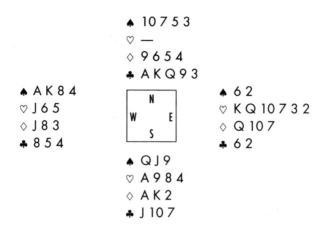

```
              ♠ 10 7 5 3
              ♡ —
              ◇ 9 6 5 4
              ♣ A K Q 9 3
  ♠ A K 8 4                    ♠ 6 2
  ♡ J 6 5          N           ♡ K Q 10 7 3 2
  ◇ J 8 3     W         E      ◇ Q 10 7
  ♣ 8 5 4          S           ♣ 6 2
              ♠ Q J 9
              ♡ A 9 8 4
              ◇ A K 2
              ♣ J 10 7
```

You lead hearts, the suit in which partner opened a weak two, and find yourself on play after two rounds of the suit.

This deal occurred in a big European tournament and the play often followed the same path for the first two tricks. It was from there that it diverged. Some Wests continued plugging away at hearts but this is silly. If East has an entry with the ◇A, the contract is down in top tricks. If not, what point does it serve to set up winners in East's hand?

A few Wests tried laying down a top spade. Their partners discouraged but there was then no time for a diamond trick. The spade switch is equally futile. If declarer were wide open in the suit, why would he keep holding up his heart stopper, especially when each discard weakens dummy's spades?

One West switched to the ◇3 and thought he had struck gold when an astute declarer let East's queen hold. Alas, East returned a diamond and the 3-3 break saw the contract home.

'How could I tell?' wailed East, 'I placed you with ◇K-J-x'. This strikes us as a fair comment. West should have led the eight of diamonds aiming to express a lack of interest in the suit.

Minor Matters

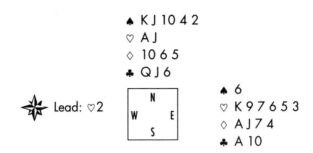

```
        ♠ K J 10 4 2
        ♡ A J
        ◇ 10 6 5
        ♣ Q J 6
                        ♠ 6
                        ♡ K 9 7 6 5 3
Lead: ♡2    N           ◇ A J 7 4
         W     E        ♣ A 10
            S
```

Dealer East
Both vul.

WEST	NORTH	EAST	SOUTH
		1♡	1♠
2♡	4♠	all pass	

Again, we present the direct rubber auction. In competition play, North might have a clever trick to show a raise to game with at least four trumps: a jump cuebid of 4♡. Of course, if he plays that, he gives up the ability to express a void or singleton heart and slam interest, so the advantage is small.

Declarer wins the heart with dummy's ace and ruffs a heart to hand. He then draws trumps with the ace and king (West has two small and you throw a heart) and calls for the ♣6.

You face two decisions here: (1) do you go up with the ace? (2) if you duck, what will you do after winning the next club?

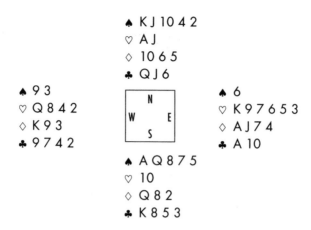

♠ K J 10 4 2
♡ A J
◇ 10 6 5
♣ Q J 6

♠ 9 3
♡ Q 8 4 2
◇ K 9 3
♣ 9 7 4 2

♠ 6
♡ K 9 7 6 5 3
◇ A J 7 4
♣ A 10

♠ A Q 8 7 5
♡ 10
◇ Q 8 2
♣ K 8 5 3

Declarer wins the first heart in dummy, ruffs a heart, draws trumps in two rounds and leads dummy's low club.

West has to hold the ◇K if you are to defeat the contract but South may well possess the ◇Q. In this case partner will presumably need the ◇9 or declarer can finesse. To avoid having to open up the frozen diamond suit you might feel tempted to grab the ♣A, but can this ever work?

If declarer has ◇Q-8-x-x and only three clubs, he will win your club return with the ♣K and cross to the ♣Q. When you show out, he will read you for four diamonds and force West, who will have a doubleton ◇K-9, to concede a ruff and discard by leading a diamond to the eight. As the cards lie, playing the ♣A gives declarer three club tricks instead of two, allowing him to throw a diamond from dummy.

You have to duck the first club and win the second. Now you must find an exit. A low diamond will not work as declarer runs this round to dummy. Cashing the ace also fails as you will be totally stuck on the next trick. The solution is to lead the jack. West captures the queen with the king and, knowing that South's fourth club is a loser, he will exit safely in clubs.

fateful Resurrection

```
                    ♠ K Q 9 5 3
                    ♡ Q
                    ◇ 8 7 3
                    ♣ J 8 4 3
                                        ♠ A 10 7 6 2
              Lead: ◇Q    ┌─────────┐   ♡ J 10 6 2
                          │    N    │   ◇ 4
                          │ W     E │   ♣ A K 5
                          │    S    │
                          └─────────┘
```

Dealer East
N–S vul.

WEST	NORTH	EAST	SOUTH
		1♠	dbl
2♠	pass	pass	4♡
all pass			

West leads the ◇Q and declarer wins with the ace. Barely pausing for thought, he advances the ♣Q to which partner follows with the ♣7. With dummy short on entries you can read this as a length signal, quite likely second highest from four to the ten or four to the nine.

If you think about it, the bidding combined with what you have already seen gives you an almost complete count on declarer's hand, both in terms of shape and high cards. This is just as well since you need to defend accurately on several tricks to come out on top. What strategy do you adopt?

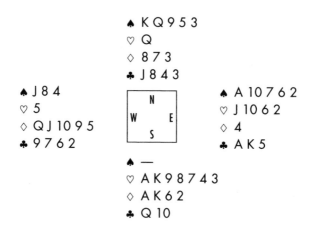

```
                    ♠ K Q 9 5 3
                    ♡ Q
                    ◊ 8 7 3
                    ♣ J 8 4 3
   ♠ J 8 4                              ♠ A 10 7 6 2
   ♡ 5             ┌─────────┐          ♡ J 10 6 2
   ◊ Q J 10 9 5    │    N    │          ◊ 4
   ♣ 9 7 6 2       │ W     E │          ♣ A K 5
                   │    S    │
                   └─────────┘
                    ♠ —
                    ♡ A K 9 8 7 4 3
                    ◊ A K 6 2
                    ♣ Q 10
```

Declarer wins partner's queen of diamonds lead with the ace and advances the queen of clubs.

It can hardly gain to duck the club since you know declarer has a doubleton. If, as seems likely, he has a seven-card heart suit headed by the ♡A-K and can come to a spade trick, a club will be his tenth trick.

Having won the club, you must play a trump. Nothing else looks attractive and you clearly want to remove dummy's entry. You can guess what is coming next: the ♠K. It seems natural to cover. Shall we see what happens?

Declarer ruffs, lays down two high trumps and leads the ♣10. You can win this and cash your master trump (keep in mind that if you duck the second club, you will be thrown in with your trump trick) but then you have to play a black card and bring dummy back to life. Declarer throws one diamond on the ♠Q and another on the ♣J to make the contract.

To prevent this from happening, you must duck the spade. South can throw one diamond but no endplay works because you now have the ♠A as an eventual exit card.

Against the Grain

```
                        ♠ A 10 2
   ✳ Lead: ◇5          ♡ 10 5
                        ◇ A K Q 6 2
                        ♣ A 8 5
♠ J 8 6 5          ┌─────────┐
♡ Q 9 6 2          │    N    │
◇ 5                │ W     E │
♣ K J 7 3          │    S    │
                   └─────────┘
```

Dealer South
Both vul.

WEST	NORTH	EAST	SOUTH
			2♡
pass	4♡	all pass	

Quite correctly, North raises South's weak two directly to game. This leaves East, who might have wished to compete, guessing whether or not North has a strong hand and keeps both of you in the dark about the quality of South's preempt.

Holding four trumps, you normally try for a forcing game rather than going for ruffs. Here the knowledge that declarer has six hearts reduces the likelihood of his losing control and neither black suit really appeals. You lead the ◇5 and under dummy's ace partner plays the ◇9, which you take as a length signal. Declarer cashes the ♡A-K, East following with the ♡J and then discarding a low spade.

Now a diamond is led towards dummy. Do you ruff? If you answer yes, what are you going to do next?

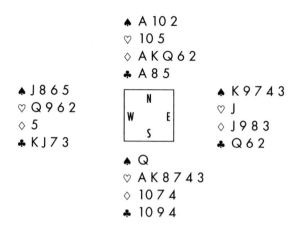

♠ A 10 2
♥ 10 5
♦ A K Q 6 2
♣ A 8 5

♠ J 8 6 5   ♠ K 9 7 4 3
♥ Q 9 6 2   ♥ J
♦ 5   ♦ J 9 8 3
♣ K J 7 3   ♣ Q 6 2

♠ Q
♥ A K 8 7 4 3
♦ 10 7 4
♣ 10 9 4

You lead a diamond to dummy's ace. Declarer takes two top trumps and then plays a diamond towards dummy.

It goes against the grain to ruff a loser, so imagine you discard on this trick. All may be well if declarer continues the suit from dummy. You can ruff, switch to a club (partner will have had several chances to signal for the suit) and overruff the fourth round of diamonds to get in to cash two clubs.

In practice, after the ♦K wins, declarer takes the ♠A and a spade ruff to play the third round of diamonds from hand. You cannot gain by ruffing this, but if you discard and then overruff the fourth diamond, you will have no side winners to cash.

Although nothing can now be done if South holds a 2-6-3-2 shape (you lack the time to set up a trick in both black suits), on the actual deal you can beat the contract if you ruff the second diamond. Knowing East would hardly have thrown a spade from ♠K-Q-x, you switch to a club. This brings you back to the winning position: you have winners to take at the point when you ruff the third round of diamonds.

Rosenberg's Rule

⁜ Lead: ♣5

♠ A J 10
♡ 6 5
♦ K J 10 6 5
♣ J 6 2

♠ Q 9 5 4
♡ 10 9 3
♦ A 3
♣ K 10 7 5

```
        N
   W         E
        S
```

Dealer South
E–W vul.

WEST	NORTH	EAST	SOUTH
			1♠
pass	2♦	pass	2♡
pass	2♠	pass	3♡
pass	4♠	all pass	

On the opponents' system, North's response at the two-level already indicates reasonable values, so he has no need to jump on the second round. However, his 2♠ just might have been false preference on a doubleton and he happily accepts South's natural game try of 3♡.

You lead the ♣5. East wins with the ♣A and returns the ♣3, declarer playing the ♣Q on the second round. You win with the ♣K and must form a plan to take two more tricks. What is it?

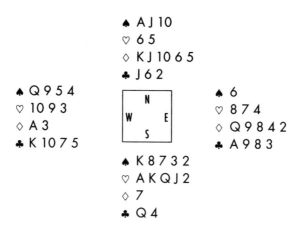

♠ A J 10
♥ 6 5
♦ K J 10 6 5
♣ J 6 2

♠ Q 9 5 4
♥ 10 9 3
♦ A 3
♣ K 10 7 5

♠ 6
♥ 8 7 4
♦ Q 9 8 4 2
♣ A 9 8 3

♠ K 8 7 3 2
♥ A K Q J 2
♦ 7
♣ Q 4

Your side cashes two club tricks against 4♠. You will cash the ♦A next. If declarer is 5-5 in the majors, then he has a singleton diamond and he may discard it on the ♣J. When the ♦A holds, you will still need one more trick.

You can guess that declarer has a two-way trump finesse and you fear he will get right. Do you see why? If trumps split 3-2 it is a toss-up, but he can only pick up ♠Q-9-x-x in your hand. You must make him believe he can cater for four trumps with East. You will do this by playing the ♠9 on the first round.

This was a good example of Michael Rosenberg's 'always play the nine unless you must' rule. It can also work here:

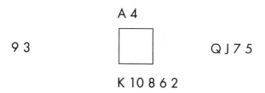

A 4

9 3

Q J 7 5

K 10 8 6 2

You must drop the nine under the ace so that declarer might put you with J-9 or a Q-9 doubleton. If not, he will finesse the ten on the second round.

Perseverance

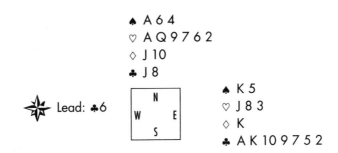

♠ A 6 4
♡ A Q 9 7 6 2
◇ J 10
♣ J 8

Lead: ♣6

♠ K 5
♡ J 8 3
◇ K
♣ A K 10 9 7 5 2

Dealer South
E–W vul.

WEST	NORTH	EAST	SOUTH
			1♠
pass	2♡	3♣	pass
pass	4♠	all pass	

North-South are playing five-card majors and South's pass over
3♣ indicates a minimum or near-minimum opening, obviously
without heart support. So, at his second turn, North bids what he
thinks they can make.

Partner leads the ♣6 and everyone follows to two rounds of
the suit. You have the lead to the next trick and feel confident
about regaining it with your king of trumps. How can you make
the most of these opportunities to dictate the play?

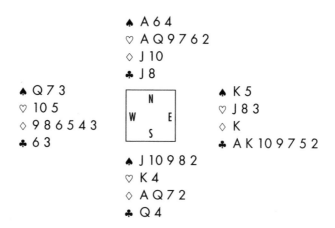

```
                    ♠ A 6 4
                    ♡ A Q 9 7 6 2
                    ◇ J 10
                    ♣ J 8
  ♠ Q 7 3                              ♠ K 5
  ♡ 10 5                               ♡ J 8 3
  ◇ 9 8 6 5 4 3                        ◇ K
  ♣ 6 3                                ♣ A K 10 9 7 5 2
                    ♠ J 10 9 8 2
                    ♡ K 4
                    ◇ A Q 7 2
                    ♣ Q 4
```

You win the first two tricks with big clubs. Three possibilities
now spring to mind: (1) continue clubs in the hope that this pro-
motes partner's trumps, (2) switch to hearts, aiming to set up a
ruff for him, and (3) try your diamond with safety in mind and
the chance of finding West with the queen.

A brief recap of the bidding indicates the folly of looking for
a heart ruff. South would have raised hearts with three, so West
cannot have a singleton. A switch to a diamond looks pretty
hopeless as well. The long heart suit in dummy means you need
to defend actively. What is the point of playing to develop a winner that partner can never get in to cash?

Your best chance is to keep plugging away at clubs. This will
lead to a trump promotion if West has at least ♠Q-7-x, ♠J-9-x or
♠Q-10. In the first case, declarer can counter by starting on
trumps with a low one off dummy. Since he has to ruff the third
club with his ♠8 (to stop West from inserting the ♠7), his only
way of getting to dummy to do so is in hearts. However, partner
will have thrown a heart and a ruff will be available after all.